INTO DARKNESS

HOW JERSEY AND ITS PEOPLE SURVIVED
FIVE YEARS OF NAZI OCCUPATION

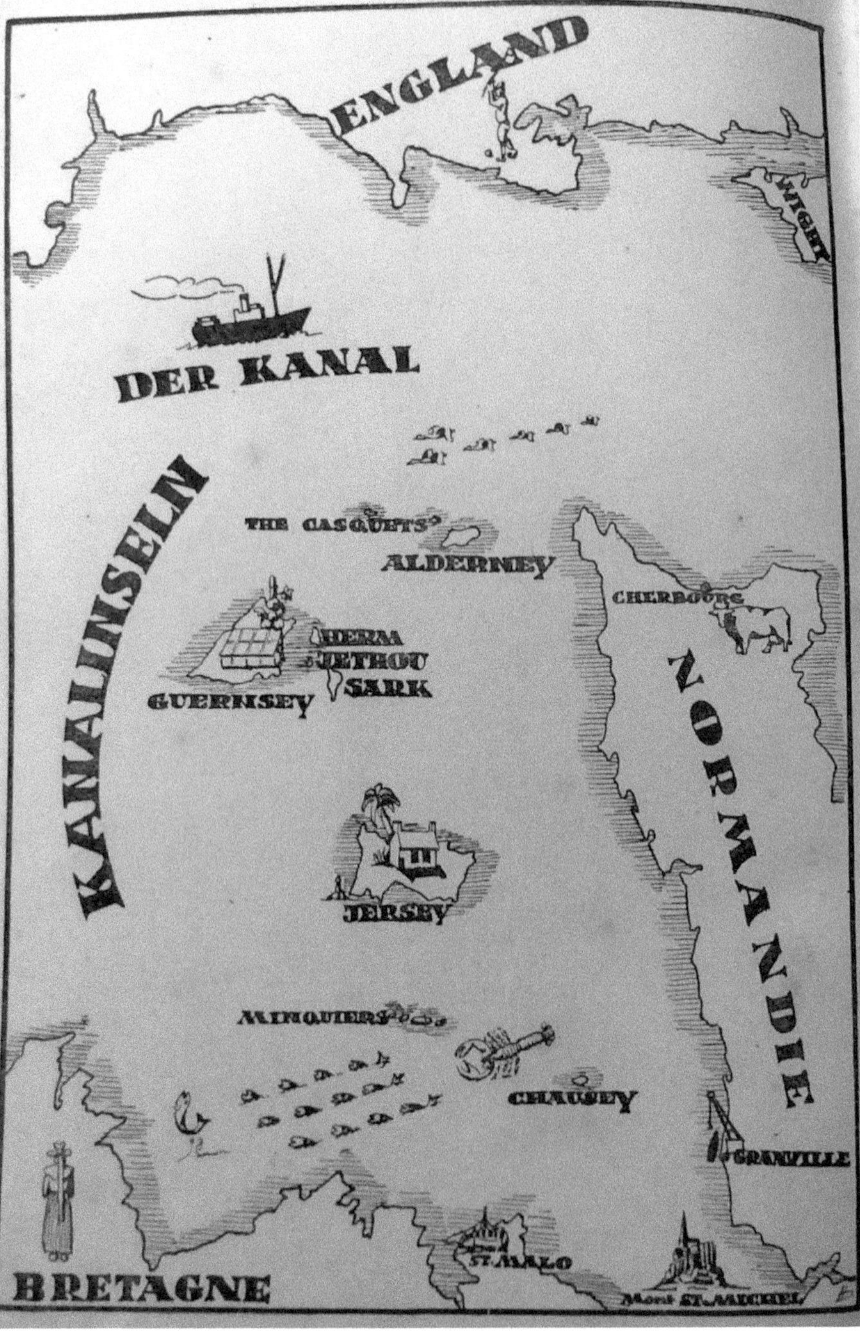

ENGLAND
WIGHT
DER KANAL
KANALINSELN
THE CASQUETS
ALDERNEY
CHERBOURG
GUERNSEY
SARK
JERSEY
NORMANDIE
MINQUIERS
CHAUSEY
GRANVILLE
BRETAGNE
ST. MALO
Mont ST. MICHEL

INTO DARKNESS

HOW JERSEY AND ITS PEOPLE SURVIVED
FIVE YEARS OF NAZI OCCUPATION

Chris Stone

INTRODUCTION BY JOHN NETTLES

Seeker Publishing in association with Jersey War Tunnels

Published in 2022 by
Seeker Publishing
Jersey, Channel Islands
in association with
Jersey War Tunnels
www.jerseywartunnels.com

Origination by Seaflower Books
www.ex-librisbooks.co.uk

Printed by CPI Group (UK) Ltd, Croydon CR0 4YY

We acknowledge with thanks permission to reproduce photographs supplied by
Jersey War Tunnels Photographic Archive

ISBN 978-1-9162118-9-6

"It would be
impertinent
for any country
that has not
suffered
occupation to
pass judgement
on one **that did**"

Anthony Eden

CONTENTS

Foreword

by John Nettles

The German Occupation

First week of July 1940. Hitler rode in triumph down the Wilhelmstrasse – and his soldiers marched onto the Channel Islands. German boots on British soil. A massive propaganda victory for the Third Reich. A disaster for the Islands. The Swastika flew over Fort Regent. The Occupation had begun and it was to last for five years, the most awful five years in the Islands' history, each one worse than the last. And how could the Islanders resist when there were so many thousand Germans and so very few of them? In any case in those first few months the Germans adopted a strangely gentle, even civilised approach to the subject population. It was going to be a model occupation with everyone behaving well. No call for resistance. But this was bound to change as the war dragged on and all the excesses of the Nazi regime found expression in these little islands as, for example the First Order Against the Jews making it a criminal offence to be a Jew, was registered in the Royal Courts. Like for example the cruel Deportation Order by which thousands of Islanders, men, women and children, were torn away from their homes and shipped to camps in Germany, leaving behind their islands which, on orders from Hitler, were to be transformed into massive and impregnable fortresses. Thousands of workers from Spain, France, Georgia, the Ukraine and Russia flooded into the islands to build the huge fortifications you can still see all about the islands. The Russian slave workers, '*untermenschen*' to the Nazis, were treated worse than dogs to the horror and disgust of the islanders. Many tried to help them, like Louisa Gould who gave refuge to an escaped slave worker. She was arrested, tried, convicted and transported to the hellish Ravensbrück concentration camp, where she died an awful death, as indeed did many others who defied the Occupation laws, by listening to the BBC or publishing an underground press.

But the worst was saved till last. Admiral Hüffmeier took command, determined to obey Hitler and defend the Islands to the death. Now if there was to be a fight to the finish many hundreds of the islanders would surely die in the Allied bombardment. It would be a bloodbath. They prayed for deliverance and deliverance came from, of all places, the bunker in Berlin, where on April 30th, Hitler shot himself and, by taking his own life, saved the lives of the islanders. For his successor and now Hüffmeier's commander, Admiral Doenitz, ordered Hüffmeier to surrender the islands unconditionally and immediately – which he did on May 9th 1945. The Occupation was over. They were free! It was the greatest of all great days in the Islands' history to be remembered as it is, with joy and thanksgiving every year – May 9th, Liberation Day in the Channel Islands.

John Nettles

A graduate in History, actor John Nettles is best known for his portrayal of Jersey's TV detective Jim Bergerac, then DCI Tom Barnaby in *Midsomer Murders*.

He wrote and presented a three-hour documentary, *The Channel Islands at War*, for the Yesterday channel.

As a writer he has written *Jewels and Jackboots*, a history of the German Occupation. He has also edited and published *The Guernsey Occupation Diaries of Douglas Ord*. A further work, on Baron von Aufsess, a chief administrator during the Occupation, is also due for release.

TIMELINE

1933

JANUARY 30th – Adolf Hitler appointed Chancellor of Germany

1934

AUGUST 19th – He becomes Führer with a policy of finding Lebensraum for the German people.

1936

MARCH 7th – German troops re-occupy the Rhineland

1939

SEPTEMBER 1st – Germany invades Poland

SEPTEMBER 3rd – Britain declares war on Germany. "I remember thinking 'Wow, how exciting', because all kids think that war's fantastic, don't they?" – Billy Reynolds

1940

MAY - JUNE – The evacuation of Dunkirk. "I served my apprenticeship of death there." – Clive Kemp

JUNE 16th - 17th – Jersey boats go to help in the evacuation of St Malo. "My pal said that as well as sundry troops they'd managed to pick up an English Lord, his wife, and her dog!" – Bob Le Sueur

JUNE 17th – The future leader of France, Charles de Gaulle, lands in Jersey to refuel en route to England. It's thought that he wrote the famous speech he delivered from the BBC the next day during that journey. "The spirit of resistance in France must not and will not go out," he says.

JUNE 20th - 27th – British soldiers leave Jersey and Guernsey, along with thousands of islanders hoping to avoid German attacks. The islands are defenceless. "I am not promising you that it will be easy. We may be hungry but we will always have our cattle and crops, our gardens, a few pigs, our sheep and rabbits." – The Dame of Sark.

JUNE 28th – The islands are bombed by the Luftwaffe. Eleven people are killed in Jersey, among them seventy eight year old John Mauger who was at the harbour when the bombers arrived. Thirty three die in Guernsey.

JUNE 30TH - JULY 1st – The first Germans land in the islands. Hauptmann Gussek is the first island commander in Jersey – twenty two years after he was held there as a prisoner during the First World War.

1941

MARCH 17th – François Scornet, a young French soldier, is shot by firing squad in St Ouens Manor after being caught trying to escape to England. "Vive Dieu! Vive la France!" are his last words.

JUNE – Work on fortifying the islands begins. "The islands must be defended. It is important to repel landing operations as soon as possible." – Guidelines for defending the islands.

JUNE 25th – Islanders are told they must now drive on the right. It causes many accidents.

SEPTEMBER – The Jersey War Tunnels. Work begins on the excavation of thousands of tons of rock beneath Meadowbank. It is originally intended as an artillery repair centre – but will eventually be taken over as a potential hospital. Four years later, the complex will still be unfinished.

OCTOBER 20th – Hitler decrees that the islands should be turned into fortresses, ready to repel any attempt to invade. The building programme will use millions of tons of cement, require the effort and lives of countless workers, and change the face of the island forever.

NOVEMBER – The first slave workers arrive to help build the fortifications. "On the opposite side of the road to our front door was shuffling, in bedraggled columns of misery, a great grey mass of humanity. These were people in the depths of exhaustion and anguish." – Bob Le Sueur.

1942

JANUARY – Work begins on labour camps in Alderney, including the infamous Lager Sylt.

JUNE 26th – The Germans order islanders to surrender their radios. Thousands do so – but many find ingenious ways to keep their precious wirelesses so they can continue to listen to the banned BBC news. "My grandmother had a large tea cosy on her bedside table, which I had always naturally assumed to be covering a teapot. But no. I lifted it away, to find a gleaming wireless tuned to the BBC which crackled quietly into life when I plugged in the cable." – Bob Le Sueur.

SEPTEMBER 15th – The order comes for non-Jersey born islanders to be deported. Horrified families are told to be ready to leave the very next day, for an uncertain fate. Over the next few weeks more than two thousand people are taken away in old coal boats to internment camps in Germany. "We were allowed one suitcase each and were told to prepare and leave a labelled trunk containing warm clothes which would be sent on later" – Michael Ginns

1943

MARCH 3rd – Canon Clifford Cohu is arrested for listening to the BBC on an illegal radio and sharing the news bulletins. He is tried, found guilty, and sent to his death in a concentration camp in Germany.

OCTOBER 2nd – The British ships HMS Charybdis and HMS Limbourne are sunk off the islands with the loss of hundreds of lives. Many bodies are washed ashore – and five thousand islanders go to a memorial service for them as a display of feeling against the Germans.

1944

MAY 19th – Louisa Gould, Harold Le Druillenec and some friends are arrested for sheltering escaped Russian slave workers. Louisa will die at Ravensbrück, Harold will be the only British survivor of Belsen. "In doing something for another mother's son, she had paid with her life." – Bob Le Sueur.

JUNE 6th – D-DAY – Islanders hear the roar of engines of countless C-47 aircraft passing overhead as they make for the drop zones of Normandy. "Me and my brother pressed our faces to the window to try to see them, the air was shaking with the noise of the planes." – Bob Le Brocq.

JUNE 17th – Hitler declares that the islands must be held at all costs. He doesn't realise that the Allies have no intention of invading, and the effort wasted on fortifying them would have been far better spent on the Atlantic Wall in France.

SEPTEMBER – The islands are cut off from resupply after the Allies take the ports on the French coast. Food runs short very quickly, but Churchill refuses permission for the Red Cross to help – for the time being. "Let 'em starve." he says – but its unclear whether he means the Germans or the islanders.

NOVEMBER – As winter looms, fuel runs out. Gas and electricity supplies are cut off. Islanders and soldiers begin to starve. Rations are cut still further.

DECEMBER – After Churchill finally relents, the SS *Vega* arrives in the islands, laden with thousands of Red Cross parcels. Luxuries such as tea, sugar and powdered milk are received by emaciated people.

1945

MARCH 7th – A German deserter, in league with the small Jersey Communist Party, blows up the Palace Hotel. There are plans for a mutiny of the troops, who feel cut off, abandoned and starving.

MARCH 8th – The Germans launch a raid on the French coast at Granville. They take several Americans prisoner.

MAY 1st – The mutineers plot fails.

MAY 8th – Thousands in the Royal Square hear Winston Churchill's radio broadcast announcing that the Channel Islands are to be freed.

MAY 9th – Liberation Day! After five long years the first British soldiers return to ecstatic scenes in the islands.

AUGUST 25th – Jersey becomes self-governing once more.

1   SHOULD WE STAY OR SHOULD WE GO?

The Channel Islands were the only part of Britain to be occupied by the Germans during the Second World War. But why did the Germans bother to take over these specks of land adrift in the English Channel, and then to fortify them so heavily? There are all sorts of reasons – from simple geography to Adolf Hitler's vanity.

Many islanders remember hearing Chamberlain's fateful declaration of war on 3 September 1939. It was a warm sunny Sunday, tourists soaked up the sun on the beaches and local people enjoyed the chance of a late summer stroll.

But others, like nineteen year-old Jerseyman Bob Le Sueur, made sure they listened to the BBC at 11.15am, when the Prime Minister said wearily that "this country is at war with Germany." Bob then ran down to the beach at First Tower, convinced this was his last chance for a swim before the Germans arrived.

But they didn't. The Phoney War had just begun, as Britain and her allies waited to see what the Führer might do. As the world held its breath, Jersey, with its long history of service to the Crown, patriotically stood ready to do its duty; hundreds of Jerseymen signed up and would eventually serve in the war.

Len Samson went down to the harbour with some friends. After two years of training he was a Sergeant Instructor with the Hampshires before volunteering for the Paras. He joined them immediately after his honeymoon.

Nineteen year-old Clive Kemp, apprenticed as a gas fitter in St Helier, lied about his age to join up with many of his friends.

'When it came to it my Dad couldn't say goodbye. He came to the pier, but he was too upset. He went up onto the top wall and waved from there. I can picture him to this day waving his hankie, and it still brings a lump to my throat.'

Clive Kemp, *Stinkers Nine Lives*

All too soon the Phoney War was over, as the Germans attacked westwards in a series of lightning manoeuvres that swept all opposition aside. Clive saw action in France and was taken off the Mole at Dunkirk, before embarking on a long war of active service.

Soon after Dunkirk, Jersey's own little ships had their particular moment of glory. Thousands of British soldiers were trapped in the port of St Malo, on the French coast to the south of Jersey. The British government asked the island if it could help. Private yachts, potato boats and even an old lifeboat sailed across to rescue as many as they could, and St Helier Yacht Club was recognised for its members gallantry.

Very soon afterwards, France surrendered. But not before a certain French tank general had made a dramatic escape – via Jersey.

Charles de Gaulle had already made a name for himself with some daring counter attacks on the Germans, and had spoken loudly of the need for France to continue to resist. As the country collapsed, on 17 June 1940 he boarded a plane in Bordeaux to take him to London, where he intended to set himself up in exile. But his aircraft had to stop somewhere to refuel. Northern France was out of the question, but the pilot knew of a little island which would be able to help…. Consequently, the future leader of France landed at Jersey airport in St Peter just before midday, and the crew began the process of preparing the aircraft for the final leg of its journey. While they waited, de Gaulle and his fellow passengers asked if they could have some lunch. They were duly taken to the Alexandra Hotel in St Peter, which is now known as the Sir George de Carteret. Well fed, they were able to get back on board and fly safely to England – after buying a case of Johnny Walker whiskey to keep them going! It's thought that de Gaulle took advantage of his time in the air to finish writing the famous broadcast which he made to his country the very next day. "France is not alone! She is not alone! She is not alone! Whatever happens, the flame of the French resistance must not be extinguished and will not be extinguished."

Many French men answered this famous call to arms, which would establish de Gaulle as the leader of the Free French – and ultimately the country's first leader after Liberation.

In Jersey, as the Germans thundered across France, there was nervousness and apprehension. Would they stop when they reached the French coast, easily visible from the east coast of the island? Those who had been following the news were sure that they would not. Jersey, a British island, was only fifteen miles away; surely Hitler couldn't resist occupying such an easy target? The army garrison had evacuated, the island was undefended, and the people who were left had to make a stark choice.

'Put that light out!' Air Raid Wardens prepared for duty, 1940

An air raid shelter protected by sandbags at Springfield

Women and children prepare to leave Jersey before the invasion

Thousands of Jersey volunteers embark to join up, 1940

One Jersey boy to join up was Leonard Eric Samson pictured here with his wife Kathleen. He became Staff Sgt, PTI, Medic - 225 Parachute Field Ambulance and was dropped into France in the first wave on D-Day.

Jersey people are, and always have been, fiercely proud of their island home. But now it was threatened by the most powerful army the world had ever seen. So what should they do?

Should they stay in their homes and farms, some of which may have been in their families for generations, stay with their families and friends, keep their jobs in their offices and fields? After all, it wasn't certain that the Germans would come; they might stop when they got to the west coast of France, and not risk an attack on British soil. Some bullishly insisted that the 'damned Hun' wouldn't dare….

But many recognised that Hitler's vanity wouldn't let him miss the chance to show the British just what he could do, and that he would love to get his hands on a genuine piece of England. So – should they go, taking the risky passage on the mailboat or smelly coal boat to Britain and safety? And if they did, what would happen to the life they left behind?

Leslie Sinel summed up the feeling of the time….

"One wasn't too sure, exactly what to do. I had bought my house. My mother-in-law was seventy. My son was just born. It was a terrible decision."

Betty Henwood's father was in England, while she was in Jersey with her mother….

"He said if you don't come off the island now I might never get back to see you again when I get leave. So we all left on the last coal boat from Jersey."

Those who wanted to go had to apply for the right permission to do so. The queues stretched for hundreds of yards, from the door of the Town Hall, all the way down Gloucester Street and down to the sea front. The lucky ones got their papers stamped and could get a boat ticket, to an uncertain future in England. One of them was sixteen year old Billy Reynolds, who got away with most of his family….

"Because we'd all left in a hurry, we couldn't take much with us, hardly more than the clothes we stood up in. I remember one well-dressed man standing next to a really nice motor car, trying to sell it or give it away to someone because he was leaving. 'Somebody give me a pound for it,' he was saying."

Billy Reynolds, *Dangerous Driving*

He had brothers and sisters in England already, and his mother determined they should join them. Leaving his elder brother George behind, Billy and his mother took a 'dirty little coal boat' across the Channel, fortified only by a bag of cherries. When they arrived they headed to his sister's in London, and Billy worked delivering fruit and vegetables from Covent Garden market. But it was the time of the Blitz, and eventually their luck ran out. His sister's home was demolished by a German bomb.

"I had nothing else left, apart from the clothes I stood up in and two shillings and sixpence in my pocket. I found my family, and we were all in tears. My sister lost everything she had."

Billy Reynolds, Dangerous Driving

The island he left behind didn't have long to wait before the Germans arrived. Hitler did indeed want to occupy Jersey, and the other Channel Islands, which was made clear in an order directly from Berlin:

'Occupation of the British Channel Islands is both urgent and necessary. Carry out local reconnaissance and execution thereof.'

But the reconnaissance they had in mind would cost many islanders their lives.

THE GERMAN BOMBING OF ST HELIER

The Home Office hadn't formally told the Germans that the Channel Islands were no longer garrisoned or defended. Not wanting to have to fight their way ashore, the Luftwaffe was given the task of assessing just how strong the defences were.

On the evening of 28 June three *Heinkel* bombers headed for Guernsey, while another three headed for Jersey.

It had been a lovely midsummer day and after finishing work Bob Le Sueur was again swimming in St Aubin's Bay – when the bombs began to fall....

"I stopped swimming, wiped the salt water from my eyes, and looked towards the direction of the intruders. They were indeed flying low over Fort Regent a mile or so to the east, and as I watched something fell from one of them. It landed with a great splash, evidently in the harbour, and then another crashed to the ground with a roar and a huge ball of fire...."

Bob Le Sueur, Growing Up Fast

Dr Averell Darling was working in the hospital, close to the harbour....

"I saw bombs begin to fall. I went through the hospital down to Casualty. And almost as soon as I got there the first victim arrived. He had a great hole blown in the side of his chest and he died within a matter of moments."

Flying over the harbour area, the Heinkel III bombers had possibly mistaken the lorries full of farm produce lined up on the quay for military vehicles, and dropped their deadly cargo. It wasn't the only place to be bombed; they also attacked the small seaside area of La Rocque. They did the same in Guernsey, killing people at the St Peter Port harbour while their machine guns terrified the survivors. Forty four Channel Islanders lost their lives that day, among them seventy eight year old Jersey man John Mauger. There was virtually no resistance. The Germans could see that the Channel Islands were theirs for the taking.

Other aircraft flew over shortly afterwards. Instead of dropping bombs, these dropped containers full of leaflets demanding that every building should display a white flag as a sign of surrender.

The island's government, the States of Jersey, held an emergency sitting while a crowd of hundreds gathered outside in the Royal Square. Among them were workmen armed with paintbrushes, and Bob Le Sueur whose office was very close by. He recalled the atmosphere of desperation and resignation….

> "Two women were standing close to me. I overheard one say to the other 'The moment this is over we must hurry home and barricade the doors. There are going to be a lot of women raped before nightfall.'"
>
> Bob Le Sueur, *Growing Up Fast*

Finally the Bailiff, Alexander Coutanche, emerged to speak to the people. There was no choice, he told them, but to surrender the island. But he reassured them….

> "I will never leave and my wife will be by my side."

As the nervous crowd began to disperse, the workmen dipped their brushes into large pots and began to paint an enormous white cross in the centre of the square.

Later that day, an Oberleutnant Kern began the Occupation by landing his Dornier at the airport and asking to speak to 'Herr Governor'. The Lieutenant Governor, the King's representative in Jersey, had already left so the Bailiff, Alexander Coutanche, had the unfortunate honour of handing the island over to its new occupiers.

Kern was soon followed by more soldiers, sailors and airmen who rapidly took over the airport, harbours and other important places across the island. Edward Le Quesne began to keep his famous Occupation diary….

> "Within an hour from the first landing, plane after plane descended at the airport and soon German soldiers in uniform were to be seen at all the principal crossroads and at various places in the town. All communication with the mainland was immediately cut and to all intents we were an island apart, even being prohibited to listening to news broadcasts from England. I went to bed that night a sad and broken man."
>
> *Diary of Edward Le Quesne, 1 July 1940*

Edward Le Quesne, born in 1882, was an elected Deputy of the States of Jersey when the war began. During the Occupation he tried to minimise the effect of German demands on his fellow islanders in his position as President of the Department of Labour. He spent time in prison for possession of a radio.

It was the same across the other Channel Islands. In little Sark, the first Germans arrived in a lifeboat they had taken in Guernsey. They had to climb up a steep hill and across the island to the home of the Dame of Sark, Cybil Hathaway, who had told the small population that she and her husband intended to stay. She did the officers the honour of receiving them with old-school English politeness and reserve, as though they were guests, and kept that form of aloof distance throughout the Occupation.

In Jersey, the islands first military commander (*Inselkommandant*) arrived, and it was something of a homecoming for him. Hauptmann Erich Gussek had been a soldier in the First World War, and was taken prisoner on the Western front. Britain had asked Jersey to accept some of its thousands of POWs, and accordingly the island built a large camp of wooden huts to house them on the sandbanks at the southern end of St Ouen's Bay. (You can still see its foundations among the undergrowth today.) Gussek had been one of the one thousand five hundred men to be held there by the time the Armistice was signed. After his country's defeat he returned to Germany, only to resume his career as a soldier. By July 1940 he was the commanding officer of No 1 Company, 216 Infantry Division – which just happened to be the unit assigned to occupy the island. Now, furnished with a highly polished Wolsely taxi, he took over the Lieutenant Governor's residence Government House, and set up the Town Hall in St Helier as his headquarters. While he was only in charge for a few months, to his credit there was no indication that he used his position to gain revenge for his ignominious accommodation a quarter of a century earlier!

For the people of Jersey though, the arrival of Hauptmann Gussek and his men signalled the beginning of five long years of Occupation.

What would you have done? Would you have stayed at home in Jersey with your family and friends, and risk being occupied – or would you have left everything behind for the safety of Britain?

Crowds wave goodbye to evacuees, June 1940

'When would they see their homes again?'

The Bombing of St Helier Harbour by Gerald Palmer

2   OCCUPIED: THE EARLY YEARS

"The pre-Occupation purveyors of rape, pillage and wholesale looting rumours were sadly disappointed when it was found that the new arrived troops went around saluting everything that moved, paying for anything they obtained in the shops, and patting small children on the head."

Michael Ginns, *Jersey Occupied*

In the days immediately after the Occupation began, islanders waited nervously for the expected rampages of the ghastly Hun. Instead, wave after wave of smiling, well-fed and well-behaved young men poured out of transport aircraft and boats keen to discover this island paradise. They laughed and smiled, and some islanders were bemused to find them 'just like us!'.

They seemed keen to make a good impression, and the island's shopkeepers in particular did very well out of them. The soldiers were happy to be in such a beautiful place, and very keen to send home souvenirs. Within a few days, the shelves of many jewellers and perfumiers in town were stripped bare by men with good manners and ready cash. Islanders were amazed that they actually *paid* for what they wanted, instead of simply taking it. Nan Le Ruez noted it in her diary....

"Cycled to town after breakfast to buy a silver watch for John's birthday. They only had five watches left, as the Germans have had them all."

Diary of Nan Le Ruez, 24 May 1941

Nan Le Ruez lived on a farm in St Peter during the Occupation. The war separated her from her fiancée Alfred, who was a Methodist missionary in Africa when the Germans invaded Jersey. Her own faith helped her to endure the worry and hardship of the next five years.

But it wasn't all rosy. A list of orders from the new rulers published in the newspaper made it clear who was in charge, and they were the first of many proclamations. The islanders would have to make some far reaching changes to the way they lived their lives.

Anyone with a car had to surrender it for possible requisition by the Germans; and listening to the BBC was *verboten*. This was the first restriction on radio listening, which would be enforced far more strictly later in the Occupation. Even at this early stage though, people were prepared to defy the orders and tune in....

"If you meet a friend, you do not ask him 'Have you listened in?' but 'Have you had a good or bad dream?'"

Diary of Edward Le Quesne, 10 July 1940

Other restrictions included a curfew – everyone had to be home by eleven o'clock at night, and the blackout rules stayed in force.

The curfew may have confused a few at first, because the island was also expected to move onto European time – meaning all the clocks had to go forward an hour.

There were also ominous signs of the hunger and want that was to come in later years. Rationing was tightly enforced. Just days after the Germans arrived, Edward Le Quesne described the situation....

"We are already existing almost on a vegetarian diet, as the allowance of meat only permits us to have sufficient for a meal of flesh once or at most twice a week. Another large consignment of potatoes has been ordered .... for immediate shipment."

Diary of Edward Le Quesne, 9 July 1940

German soldiers were soon nicknamed 'Greenfly' because of the distinctive colour of their uniforms.

In common with other occupied countries, islanders were required to own, and carry at all times, an identity card. These carried basic information of name, age, etc, plus a photo of the bearer. In recent years these pictures have become iconic images of the Occupation, the grim unsmiling faces in black and white a reminder of the repression and control the cards represented. To be found without your card, particularly after curfew, would at least result in a visit to College House to be disciplined, or possibly even prison. Losing one was a serious misdemeanour and you would have to appeal to the authorities for a replacement. Notably, they weren't administered by the Germans, but the islands civil service, and an official named Clifford Orange was known to be very strict about their correct use. He was also responsible for recording people of different nationalities in the island, and was strongly criticised after the war for agreeing to identify Jewish people clearly on their documents.

Tons of Jersey produce, together with many requisitioned cars, were shipped off the island to the continent to supply the needs of the all conquering German army. In fact, later in the war as he drove across France with the Guards Armoured

Division, Billy Reynolds happened upon what he believed was his brother's car, clumsily painted green over its original maroon body.

Many of the finer sports cars stayed on the island, as the German officers took a shine to the expensive Jaguars and MGs. Soon they were roaring around the island with little care for the rules of the road, which led to several accidents, as Philip Le Sauteur noted in his diary....

> "Another civilian has paid the penalty of getting in the way of a Jerry car. I don't know what the score of road deaths is for the past eleven moths, but I reckon it is as high as the previous eleven years."
>
> *Diary of Philip Le Sauteur,* 26 May 1941

Philip Le Sauteur ran a builders merchants during the Occupation, and frequently clashed with the Germans over supplies of concrete and other materials. His wide contacts meant he heard a lot of details of what was happening in the island.

He was unaware of it at the time, but the 'civilian' killed in this accident was a Jersey Great War hero. Colonel Walter Stocker had been in charge of the Jersey Pals, a group of islanders who had volunteered and served together across the Western Front. He had retired in Jersey, and remained there at the beginning of the next war to face his former foes when they invaded. But on that day in 1941, coming out of a building almost directly opposite the Town Church on Hill Street, he was hit by a car driven by a German and died of his injuries.

Soon the Germans realised they had to do something about the mounting casualty list. But rather than simply driving more carefully, they announced without warning that everyone should now drive on the right. The notices appeared in the Evening Post on Monday 23 June 1941, and the order remained in place until the end of the war.

But as well as all of these restrictions, there was one even more pressing question which concerned every Jersey person at the beginning of the Occupation. It was simply: "How should I behave towards them?"

They were polite, well spoken and not aggressive. They paid for what they wanted from shops, and even when they requisitioned cars they issued strictly correct receipts. The dilemma of Bob Le Sueur's mother as she caught a bus in the early weeks of the Occupation sums up many people's experience....

> "She came through the front door greatly flustered.... She explained that the bus had been full, so she had been standing up with all her shopping in her

arms until a bump in the road caused her to drop her parcel on the floor. A young German soldier got up, picked it up, offered her his seat and handed her parcel back. 'But what should I have done?' she asked, 'I felt obliged to thank him, which meant looking him in the eye and being grateful to him, and surely that's not the right thing to do?'"

Bob Le Sueur, *Growing Up Fast*

> What would you have done if you had been Bob's mother? Would you have smiled and thanked the soldier for his politeness? If not – how would you have responded?

It wasn't until the arrival of the slaves in 1942 that the attitude of many Jersey people changed from passive acceptance of their situation to outright disgust and hatred for the Germans. In fact, many determined to carry on with their lives as far as possible as if nothing untoward was happening.

A CHILD'S EYE VIEW

Even children weren't able to escape the German influence. It was ordained that every school pupil should learn the German language, and inspectors would appear to make sure teachers were complying. Few wished to fill their children's heads with an alien vocabulary, and some came up with ingenious ways to subvert the order. Colin Borny, for example, remembered a young Irish teacher who taught every child in her class one single word of German each. When the *Inspektor* arrived, her plan came into action….

"The teacher would rapidly, and apparently randomly, call a boy's name and give him an English word to be translated. My cue was to be ready when she called 'Coutanche, window?' and he would reply '*Fenster*, Miss.' Then, 'Borny, pencil?' and I would reply '*Bleistift*, Miss', and so on around the class. Herr *Inspektor* would congratulate us, click his heels, salute, proclaim 'Heil Hitler!', and leave."

Many young boys in particular enjoyed the regular spectacle of German marching bands and the columns of soldiers stamping along behind them. Many youngsters joined in, although not always with happy results….

Brian Rondel lived up Mont Felard….

"One day the Germans were marching up and down the road and of course as kids do we decided to march with them. But they set a dog on us and I got bitten on the bottom. I can remember going home and dropping my trousers and my mother putting iodine on the spot which wasn't very comfortable! Another friend of mine was bitten on the knee. The funny thing was, they never bit a German…."

For many youngsters it was all a bit of a novelty, a game whose consequences they didn't always understand. Young Alan Rabet was playing under an old lorry in his father's barn when he came across a hidden radio – just as a German patrol came by to make a search….

"I thought I'd better tell Dad I've found a radio. He was talking to a German at the time, and I rushed up and I was pulling at his trousers, yelling at him, 'Dad, Dad, I've found a radio!' My Dad was not amused but thankfully the German didn't realise what was going on!"

The privations suffered by the islanders as the rations became shorter and the nights grew longer at the end of 1944 were particularly hard for children as they needed good protein and vitamins to grow. Academic studies suggest that young people during and after the Occupation were lighter and shorter than the previous average, despite many parents giving up their own rations to feed their children. The sweets and treats that we now take for granted simply didn't exist for them, and they like everyone else had to exist on bland, undercooked root vegetables and bread filled with sawdust. When the SS *Vega* arrived with its consignment of Red Cross parcels it must have seemed like all their Christmases had come at once.

Not all children remember the Occupation as a time of trial though. For those with imagination and the will to explore it could be a time of excitement, of novelty, of freedom and challenge. While parents worked hard to find food, children were sent to glean from the fields or find scraps of wood for the fire. There was adventure to be had.

Brian Raffray looks back on his youth with great affection, especially the games he played with the soldiers. He lived opposite Springfield, the sports stadium in St Helier where the Germans used to train….

"My Occupation was the best years of my life, I'm sure of it. I played international football against the Germans, and how many boys can say that's what happened to them?…. If they wanted extra men, us boys made up the teams to play. And I scored a goal against the Germans, which I've treasured all my life!"

Nan Le Ruez

Edward Le Quesne

Philip Le Sauteur

Translation of a Communication addressed to the Governor of the Isle of Jersey.

1st July, 1940.

To the Chief of the Military and Civil Authorities

Jersey (St. Helier).

1. I intend to neutralize military establishments in Jersey by occupation.

2. As evidence that the Island will surrender the military and other establishments without resistance and without destroying them, a large White Cross is to be shown as follows, from 7 a.m. July 2nd, 1940.

   a. In the centre of the Airport in the East of the Island.
   b. On the highest point of the fortifications of the port.
   c. On the square to the North of the Inner Basin of the Harbour.

   Moreover all fortifications, buildings, establishments and houses are to show the White Flag.

3. If these signs of peaceful surrender are not observed by 7 a.m. July 2nd, heavy bombardment will take place.

   a. Against all military objects.
   b. Against all establishments and objects useful for defence.

4. The signs of surrender must remain up to the time of the occupation of the Island by German troops.

5. Representatives of the Authorities must stay at the Airport until the occupation.

6. All Radio traffic and other communications with Authorities outside the Island will be considered hostile actions and will be followed by bombardment.

7. Every hostile action against my representatives will be followed by bombardment.

8. In case of peaceful surrender, the lives, property, and liberty of peaceful inhabitants are solemnly guaranteed.

   The Commander of the German Air Forces in Normandie,

   _____ General

The States have ordered this Communication to be printed and posted forthwith, and charge the inhabitants to keep calm, to comply with the requirements of the Communication and to offer no resistance whatsoever to the occupation of the Island.

These leaflets were dropped by aircraft over the island

Surrender: the first Germans take charge at the airport

The Bailiff and Attorney General discuss terms

The occupiers came by air and by sea to take control in a show of force

The Swastika flies from the Town Hall - the new German HQ

Posed for propaganda purposes - the soldier and the bobby outside the Town Hall

The first German troops on British soil take holiday snaps…

…after an easy victory

Corbière

St Ouen's Bay

St Aubin's Fort

West Park Pavillion

For the next five years the only guests here would be German.
Many island hotels were requisitioned by the occupiers

St Aubin's Harbour

3 FORTRESS JERSEY: CONCRETE AND STEEL

When the Germans first arrived in Jersey and the other Channel Islands, they looked about for ways to fortify them against a possible counter attack by the British.

The only real fortifications on the islands were centuries old. The great castles such as Mont Orgueil and Elizabeth harkened back to days of swords and halberds; while the Martello towers dotted about the coast were a more recent response to the threat of French invasion. They were tall towers with thick granite walls and loopholes for cannon or musket.

While of historic interest they were evidently unsuitable for the firepower of modern warfare, and work got underway quickly to adapt some of them as far as possible. They were called *Feldwache* and were often manned by little more than a couple of men with rifles or machine guns. Other defensive positions were hastily thrown up along the most vulnerable areas of coast, for example St Aubin's Bay and St Ouen's Bay. The assumption on Hitler's part was that Britain would be so incensed by the seizure of her territory that she would surely strike back. On 3 October, the Order for the Defence of the Channel Islands said….

> 'The islands have to be defended. It is important to repel landing operations as soon as possible and either take the enemy prisoner or throw him back into the sea by immediate counter-attack'.

The first Germans had to buy as many tourist maps of the island as they could find, because they had arrived with virtually no maps of their own. They relied on these to plan where to build their first defences.

Work accelerated and the first coastal artillery began to be installed. About six thousand labourers from Spain were the first to come to the island to take on the huge projects of concrete and steel around the island's coast. They weren't slaves, or treated as such, but housed in camps at La Moye and Grouville. While they certainly weren't free men, they were able to leave their camps and interact with local people.

They soon became popular with some local men's outfitters. While the Germans had bought up much of their supplies of cloth and ready clothes, they had turned their noses up at the traditional British bowler hats on display which seemed destined to languish forgotten in the shop window. The Spanish workers soon realised that the hats were perfect protection for their heads as they dug underground, and they quickly bought what stocks there were from their meagre pay.

The Germans appealed for local labour. They cunningly offered any local man more than the going rate to help to dig the foundations and pour the concrete of the bunkers and gun platforms. Many found the lure of easy money hard to resist, especially those with families or other commitments. One of the first large scale excavations began at Noirmont point on the south west corner of the island, a place which dominates the southern approaches to St Helier.

Things started to accelerate the following April, when Hitler considered the islands in a more strategic way. They were, in effect, stationary gun platforms which could be used to block the western coast of France and the route between the Cherbourg peninsula and the ports of St Malo and western Brittany. Any attack there would divert attention away from his plan for his next conquest in Russia. Consequently he ordered that a whole division should garrison the island and 319 Infantry Division found itself the new guardians of Jersey. Soon the islands harbour was busy with boats full of guns and ammunition….

> "As a result of *Generalmajor* Schmetzer's tactical survey, it was…. realised that guns of sufficient calibre and range would not only protect the islands against attack, but would also cover the entire Bay of St Malo, thus obviating the need to fortify the west coast of the Contention Peninsula. As this idea appealed to Hitler, he ordered the transfer of vast quantities of coastal artillery to the Channel Islands with the result that by the end of 1941 the German's artillery reserves in Western Europe were exhausted."
>
> Michael Ginns, *Jersey Occupied*

This pilfering of the stockpile of German weapons was a foretaste of things to come. Soon vast quantities of resources would be diverted to fortify the islands, which could otherwise have been used to build bunkers and gun positions along the French coast.

It's estimated that the bunkers, tunnels and defences in the Channel Islands used up about a twelfth of all the concrete expended on Hitler's Atlantic Wall.

The first major medical facility in Jersey was set up at La Haule Manor hotel, and several others were scattered around the island. But plans were already in place to build a complete hospital underground, in space tunnelled out of the rock in one of the island's valleys. Originally it was meant to be at West Mount, close to the General Hospital in St Helier. When they realised this was impracticable, their attention turned to a recently started artillery storage tunnel at Meadowbank in St Lawrence, which was conveniently protected by its natural cover and a safe distance from the beach. 'Ho8' would become a *Hauptverbandzplatz* or Casualty Receiving Station, and would eventually form a series of interlocking tunnels full of hospital beds and medical equipment, all of which were destined never to be used. It is now known as The Jersey War Tunnels.

By the end of 1941, the occupiers had realised two things. Firstly, if it did become necessary to repel an invasion of the islands they would need to build bigger and better fortifications. And secondly, that the supply of men willing to do the work was far too small. They needed more manpower, and their solution was simple and brutal. They imported slave workers from the territories they had conquered in the east, where their treatment of those they regarded as *untermensch* was far worse than any Jersey people had experienced.

The planned extension of the fortifications and garrison duties of the Channel Islands was expected to require 36,000 men, an extraordinary diversion of manpower for a handful of small islands. The full plan was never realised though, and only about 10,000 soldiers actually came to Jersey. It still meant that one person in every five on the island was in uniform.

THE PRINCIPAL AREAS OF DEFENCE

On such small islands, it was evident that any serious attack had to come mainly from the sea. Jersey is not an even shape; the southern coast rises very little from sea level, and the gently sloping beaches of St Aubin's Bay make it a perfect landing ground. Similarly St Ouen's bay on the west coast offers miles of empty golden sand.

The north on the other hand is more easily defended, dominated by tall imposing cliffs tumbling down to narrow rocky beaches and deeper water.

To defend the island then, the workers and slaves threw up more than two hundred concrete buildings around the coast, as well as tunnels and communication centres inland. By the end of the war St Aubin's Bay and St Ouen's Bay in particular were dominated by anti-tank walls, huge bunkers with machines guns and artillery, and further back more bunkers for personnel and ammunition.

Many of the bunkers directly on the beach had guns that were angled to fire across the sand, rather than out to sea. Well hidden, they could wait until any invader had landed before raking them with enfilade fire and destroying them before they could make their way inland. One such was built at First Tower, a kilometre or so west of St Helier along the sea front. The Germans chose to site it almost directly in front of the existing Martello Tower, protecting a road leading inland. It was right in front of Bob Le Sueur's house on The Avenue, and he watched from his upstairs bedroom window as the workers smashed apart the beautiful granite slipway and dug foundations for a Type 631 bunker with a Czechoslovakian gun. The siting of the bunker would have serious consequences for his social life, as it was surrounded by a barbed wire barrier which came down an hour before curfew and blocked access to his front door. It meant he had to leave any social occasion an hour before his friends, and he often had to rely on the good humour of the guards to let him through if he was a few minutes late.

The island's high points were transformed by lookout towers and heavy gun emplacements, which could fire for miles out to sea and threaten any naval ships foolhardy enough to come into range.

The headlands at Noirmont, Corbière and Les Landes became huge building sites for the multi storey observation towers which are still visible from miles out to sea. The 15.5cm guns which accompanied the Les Landes battery were crewed by a hundred men and could fire on any vessel coming from the direction of Guernsey.

Even the old castles were transformed by added gun positions and lookout towers that were cleverly camouflaged to make them appear part of the original structure.

On open areas, and around defence works, barbed wire and trenches were ready to repel attack – and all over the island warning signs appeared with a simple skull and crossbones and the message 'Achtung Minen!'

The Germans laid more than 65,000 mines in Jersey. That's nearly 1,500 *per square mile*.

In March 1944, shortly before the D-Day invasion, Hitler decreed that the islands were to be considered 'fortresses', and that the garrisons should prepare to fight to the last man and last bullet. Old French tanks, captured in the invasion of 1940, had been brought to Jersey and prepared for action near possible beachheads. One of their main camps was on land now occupied by the Lavender Farm in St Brelade, next to the railway line which could ferry workers or soldiers from town to the west coast.

By the time the Allies were ready to make their attempt to liberate Europe, the Channel Islands had been turned into formidable obstacles, bristling with armaments and ready to fight.

But every gun and bunker in Jersey, Guernsey and the other islands represented tons of concrete and steel which could have been used to make defences in Normandy. As it turned out, they waited in vain for an invasion which never came.

Surrounding the island with mines, bunkers, artillery and tanks

Jersey quickly became a fortress following Hitler's orders

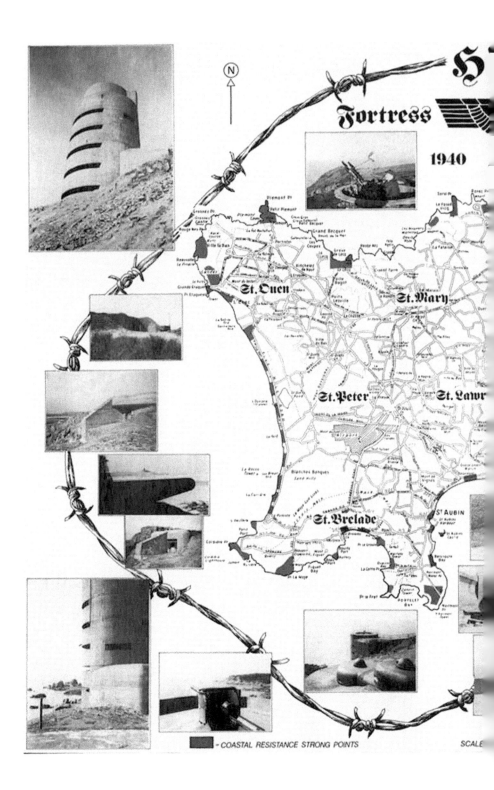

Fortress

1940

St.Ouen

St.Mary

St.Peter

St.Lawr

St.Brelade

St AUBIN

- COASTAL RESISTANCE STRONG POINTS

SCALE

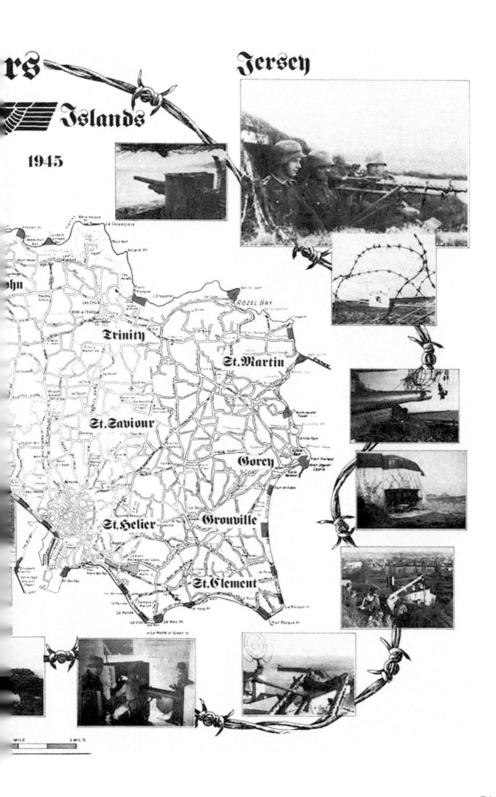

rs
Islands
1945

Jersey

Trinity

St.Martin

ROZEL BAY

St.Saviour

Gorey

St.Helier

Gronville

St.Clement

The occupiers prepare to defend the island

4 THE WAR TUNNELS: EXPLOSIVES AND EXHAUSTION

In September 1941 the war was going well for Germany. The invasion of Russia had been a staggering success, and her troops were heading for Moscow. The occupied countries of Europe were supplying resources to fuel her war effort, and America was still officially neutral.

Meanwhile Hitler was determined to hold on to the small parts of the British Isles that he had managed to capture. Work was underway to make Jersey an impregnable outpost of the Reich, and a peaceful valley in St Lawrence was chosen to house a series of tunnels to store artillery supplies. The Führer had made it clear in his latest orders that there should be plenty of safe accommodation for shells and guns which could be brought out to defend the island when the British invaded. The official name for any defensive tunnel complex was *Höhlgangsanlage*, and fourteen were planned at strategic places around the island where steep valleys would offer natural cover but quick access to the beach.

The St Lawrence tunnel was named *Höhlgangsanlage* 8, commonly abbreviated to Ho8, and it was designated an *Artillerieunterkunft* or Artillery Quarters. It would require easy access from the road, a high, wide entrance and spaces inside large enough to hold and manoeuvre lorries, ammunition carriers and large guns.

The early exploratory work was led by a military expert, *Oberleutnant* Dr Walter Klüpfel, a geologist in the island's Fortress Engineers. Two companies eventually got the task of digging the tunnels, one from each side of the valley. *Gremmich* dug from the Meadowbank side, which is where the main entrance is, and *Karl Plötner* from the opposite side known as Cap Verd.

While progress was slow to begin with, when the first slave workers arrived in 1942 it speeded up and the small road leading up the valley became clogged with men, machines and materials.

The work was dangerous, noisy and dark; the technique was simple, noisy and hazardous. It involved drills, explosives – and raw manpower.

First the drill operators would bore three metre long holes into the rock face in front of them in a semi-circle shape similar to a rainbow. Then others would push explosive charges down the holes, which were set off to blow the rock out in a rough arch. Then it was the turn of those with the hardest job – to remove all the loose rock and shovel it into barrows or temporary railway trollies, to be taken to the exit and disposed of. A 60cm gauge railway was installed to run as close to the working face as possible.

The ceiling was unstable and liable to collapse at any time, as other workers tried to shore it up with lengths of old telegraph pole held together by metal ties known as 'prop dogs'. Labouring often in near darkness, they excavated around 14,000 tons of rock to make the basic outline of the tunnels.

"…. we were thin, exhausted, dressed in torn clothes and blue with cold. The worksite was a huge labyrinth of tunnels. I was terrified. It smelt like a grave. It was hard to believe all these tunnels had been dug by the weakening hands and legs of these slaves."

Vasilly Marempolsky, quoted in Michael Ginns' *Jersey Occupied*

Most of the rock that was dug out of the tunnels was dumped close by, along the Cap Verd valley at the back entrance to the tunnels.

Once the outline of the tunnel had been blasted and excavated, other workers poured concrete to level the floor. That had to be done skilfully, because it had been designed always to slope slightly towards the tunnel entrance, to allow the complex to drain effectively. The channel on the floor, now covered with wooden boards, carried the run off.

To concrete the walls, they stacked wooden planks along the sides of the tunnels and poured the mixture in from above – you can still see the marks from where the planks were taken away once it had dried. The wood work for this and other tunnels was made at the joinery works at Five Oaks and transported to the site.

The ceilings were more complicated to cover. They built scaffolds against the walls to support large curved wooden frames. Workers on the scaffold could then shovel the concrete into the frames, then wait for it to set before completing the next section until the whole arch was complete. All 4,000 tons of concrete in the tunnels had to be carted in and shovelled by hand.

So who were the men who did this backbreaking, dirty and dangerous work?

The first were around a hundred political prisoners from around the Reich, brought to the island from France and housed in a camp at Fort Regent in St Helier. They joined German engineers and army construction battalions to begin digging the huge entrance archway. But just a month after it began, Dr Fritz Todt visited Jersey – and realised that in order for the island to be fortified to the Führer's specifications it would need far more manpower.

Dr Fritz Todt (his surname appropriately enough, means 'Dead' in English), was a senior Nazi civil engineer. He had been responsible for the *autobahn* road system which gave work to thousands of Germans and began the country's economic recovery in the 30s. Later he helped to design the fortifications of the *Westwall* which defended the heartland of Germany. He eventually became head of his own huge department, the *Organisation Todt*, which used foreigners and slaves to build bunkers and war facilities across occupied Europe. He died in a plane crash in 1942, just a few months after visiting Jersey.

As work began to intensify, more and more slaves and forced labourers were brought to the island. About one thousand two hundred Ukranian, Polish and Russian slaves joined those from other European countries, conscripts from France and North Africa, and Republican Spaniards in wielding the tools and carting the rubble at Ho8. Some described how the work was so hard that it took two of them to use a shovel. Poorly fed and harshly treated, most of them lived in a camp on Goose Green Marsh, a short march from their workplace.

The Germans even imported some Italians after their country surrendered in 1943. They were experts in bricklaying and plastering, and helped with some of the finishing work. They had help from some local Jersey plasterers who were paid up to £12 a week, four times the islands regular wage.

It's no surprise that there were many accidents. At least 22 men died in building the tunnels. For years it was assumed any bodies were simply tipped into the concrete, but in fact they were buried at the Strangers Cemetery at West Mount. Others weren't recovered, and were left under rock falls in sections which had to be abandoned.

ARE THE TUNNELS HAUNTED?

The historian Joe Mière worked at the Tunnels for many years. He always insisted they were haunted by the ghost of an *Organisation Todt* overseer, dressed in a khaki uniform. Joe often saw the figure walking the tunnels, and it was also seen by a couple in a car who had parked outside one night.

As the fortunes of war changed for the Nazis, so did plans for Ho8. By the end of 1943 it was clear that the Allies would have to attempt a landing in Europe, and many of the slave workers were shipped back to the continent to help with building defences there. Ho8 still wasn't finished, but now had a different purpose. Instead of storage for artillery and ammunition, the Germans decided it was an ideal location to look after soldiers who had been wounded in action either in Jersey or on the continent. It would be converted to house medical wards where casualties could be brought for treatment before being sent to hospital – or back to the front line.

But a medical facility has completely different requirements to those of an artillery storage site, and the Germans had to bring in more specialist workers to lay out wards, operating theatres and other essential facilities to convert it into a fully functioning *Hauptverbandsplatz* or Main Casualty Receiving Station. Whole galleries were divided and repurposed, and yet more vital stores were brought to the island from Europe where they would soon be sorely needed.

More resources were used to prepare and supply areas for storage and communications, as they expected to look after up to five hundred patients at a time. They added air conditioning, gas proof doors and a kitchen, but other, unfinished sections had to be abandoned.

After the Allied landing in Normandy in June 1944, the garrison in Jersey and the medical staff at Ho8 waited with bated breath to see if their skills and newly furnished facilities would be called into action. They prepared to take casualties from the Normandy battlefields, and rehearsed how they might defend against invaders landing on the island's beaches.

But despite all the work, all the suffering and deaths, Ho8 was never used. Jersey was cut off after the liberation of Normandy and Brittany, as the Allies pushed the retreating Germans eastwards. Historians have speculated that perhaps some survivors of the siege of St Malo in 1944 may have been brought there, but records say these men were taken to the main hospital in St Helier. It's more likely that Ho8 was being kept ready for an expected invasion of Jersey – which never came. As 1944 wore on it became clear that Jersey and the other Channel Islands had been cast adrift by Hitler and his strategists, and the resources tied up there had been wasted. Ho8 was never completed and like all the other tunnels, bunkers, minefields and barbed wire, had become an irrelevance.

After the Occupation ended, locals and visitors were keen to explore the bunkers and tunnels that had been left empty. Whether it was scavenging schoolboys looking for souvenirs or grown ups trying to make sense of what had happened to their island, they started with lamps and torches to discover what had been hidden behind the metres of thick concrete.

In at least one case that led to tragedy, as rumours persisted of tunnels crammed with guns and other treasures. In 1962 two boys were killed by fumes from a fire as they searched a nearby tunnel complex, Ho2.

The British Army took charge of Ho8, as well as the other tunnels and defensive sites. Within a year it had been cleared of anything of importance, and visitors could come to have a look around. On 9 May 1946, the first anniversary of the Liberation, Military guides escorted them though the main entrance archway and into the dimly lit passages. It was so popular that it caused traffic jams as hundreds of islanders blocked the roads heading into the St Lawrence valley. The states eventually realised that this could be a great money spinner, and began to charge sixpence a ticket for admission. When the site passed into private hands, it stayed open, was developed as a visitor attraction, and was known for years as the *German Underground Hospital*.

Now the Jersey War Tunnels, the site is dedicated to preserving, recording and presenting an accurate account of the German Occupation of Jersey.

THE JERSEY WAR TUNNELS IN FIGURES

- Officially named Höhlgangsanlage 8 – or Ho8 for short
- More than one thousand metres, or one kilometre, long; enough to fit more than one hundred coaches end to end
- Fifty metres underground
- Workers excavated fourteen thousand tons of rock by hand; that's nearly eight thousand cubic metres
- They poured four thousand tons of concrete to make the ceilings, walls and floors
- They laid four hundred thousand bricks
- At least twenty two men died in accidents and explosions
- The tunnels took four years of work – and were still unused and unfinished when the war ended

Dr Fritz Todt, the architect of the Nazi defences, examining the plans for Jersey on a visit to the island

The main entrance to Höhlgangsanlage 8, now The Jersey War Tunnels

Work begins. Major Heide outside Ho8 before it has been
shaped and lined with concrete. Note the railway tracks

Workers outside the Cap Verd entrance to Ho8

Slaves with overseers

Officers watch slave workers dig bunker foundations

Slaves outside their hut

Note the threadbare clothing

5   TAKEN: ISLANDERS DEPORTED

"Oh, it is shocking, one can hardly believe that such a thing has come to pass.
There is no word to describe the cruelty and beastliness of the Germans….
it is too dreadful, one can hardly think."
Diary of Nan Le Ruez, 15 September 1942

On the 15th September 1942, hundreds of Jersey families were told they had a matter of hours to pack some belongings and get down to the harbour. They were to be 'evacuated and transferred to Germany', according to the notices which appeared without warning in the *Evening Post*.

But why? Why did Hitler want to imprison mothers, children, and old men?

They weren't Jews, or criminals, or any of the other social groups loathed by the Nazis. In fact, it all began in Iran – then known as Persia.

At the start of the war Persia was a neutral country but its geographical location soon made it a place of strategic importance for both the Axis and the Allies. Its northern border was with Russia, and when Hitler launched Operation Barbarossa in June 1941 the Allies were concerned that Persia could be used as a base for German spies. British troops invaded and they rounded up all the Germans they could find.

Women, children and the elderly were allowed to go back to Europe, while the men were separated out. Some of those ended up in Russian prison camps, while others were sent to live out the war in India. They made an exception for Jewish Germans, who were allowed to stay.

Adolf Hitler had a habit of demanding retribution for any actions taken against what he considered to be the interests of the German Volk. The humiliation of having his people incarcerated struck deeply, and he intended to strike back in kind. His first move was to ask the authorities in Jersey and the other islands to compile a list of all islanders, to include details of their place of birth.

His intention was that any men aged between 16 and 70 who were not native to the Channel Islands, *and their families*, should be deported to the Pripet marshes in the Ukraine.

Unaware of the reasons behind such a request, the Jersey authorities drew up the necessary list; but for almost twelve months nothing further happened. In

September 1942 Hitler found out that the people of Jersey were still safe at home, and demanded immediate action.

The Bailiff, Alexander Coutanche, was summoned to a meeting with the islands military commander, *Oberst* (Colonel) Friedrich Knackfuss on the 15th September. Knackfuss told him that the first deportees must be ready to leave *the following day*, and advertisements were already in the newspaper to warn people. They said simply that the chosen islanders would be taken 'to Germany'. Knackfuss wanted the island authorities, particularly the constables, to choose who should go first. Coutanche, surprised and outraged, said that no Jersey constable should bear that responsibility – and that he himself would resign if the Germans insisted.

Knackfuss relented on the matter of the constables, but insisted that the deportations should go ahead. In the event, parish officials accompanied German soldiers to the homes of hundreds of people that very day, and warned them that they had just a few hours to pack some belongings and be ready to be taken away.

Across the island, families were faced with an almost impossible dilemma – 'What should we take – and what should we leave behind?'

And of course there was the terrible question which none of them could answer; 'Where are we being taken to?'

'Imagine it', wrote Philip Le Sauteur in his diary, 'being called on just to walk out and leave everything, especially one who has reached the autumn of life'.

Edward Le Quesne described in his diary as a terrible day for Jersey. 'After a sleepless night', he wrote, 'I fear I broke down on many occasions'.

The parishes of Jersey have come in for criticism of the way they helped to administer various German directives but in particular the deportation orders of 1942. Many found it appalling that Jersey honorary police or other parish officials were the ones who went knocking on doors and telling the occupants that they had to be ready to leave, often with just a few hours notice. Local authorities had also helped to draw up the lists of those who weren't born in the island, following German orders.

Others though were more understanding. Bob Le Sueur wrote....

"If it had to happen, the constables thought, we must make it as painless as possible. It was surely better to have the knock on the door and a sympathetic explanation from someone you knew and trusted, than a faceless German soldier issuing a cold hearted order."

Bob Le Sueur, *Growing Up Fast*

His friends the Dunns were among those given just a few hours to be at the harbour. He helped them prepare for their journey to who knows where, searching fruitlessly for a teddy bear belonging to their youngest daughter. The next day he met them at the harbour, where they and hundreds like them prepared to be herded aboard a rust-bucket boat named La France and away from their island home. The children looked huge, because they were wearing several layers of clothes to make just a little more room in their overstuffed cases. But he was struck very much by the British *sang froid*….

> "Somehow, collectively and without any need for discussion, not a single person gave in to their feelings of fright or injustice. It was extraordinary. Even the youngest children stood quietly, holding their mother's and father's hands and watching the bustle with wide eyes.
> I had been inclined to laugh at the expression 'a stiff upper lip', a relic of the old days of the Raj and the British Empire, but by God I saw it that day and I cannot think of it now without great emotion."
>
> Bob Le Sueur, *Growing Up Fast*

The future Occupation historian Michael Ginns was one of those transported from the harbour on a later sailing, at the age of fourteen. One of his strongest memories was of a German sailor with tears in his eyes who spoke to him as the boat sailed. "I wish to apologise for what is being done to you." he said. "This is not correct." Michael always remembered with a tear that very human gesture, which began his lifelong commitment to reconciling the islanders with their erstwhile occupiers.

As the final reluctant passengers embarked and La France prepared to sail, hundreds of islanders made their way up to the side of Mount Bingham, where they had a clear view of the decks. The deportees saw them, and surged over to their side of the boat. Then, says Bob Le Sueur, 'the singing began'. The crowd on land sang those impossibly poignant wartime songs, such as 'We'll Meet Again' and 'Blue Birds', and the people on the deck joined in, as the boat slipped its moorings and sailed away. The Germans knew that the Jersey people could only have heard these songs by listening to illegally held wirelesses.

As the ship passed out of the harbour and away past Elizabeth castle into the unknown, emotions were running high and scuffles broke out between some young Jersey men, powerless to save their friends, and German patrols who had been sent to calm the situation.

> "…. large crowds assemble around Mount Bingham and the biggest patriotic demonstrations since the Occupation take place; this prompts German patrols to clear the roadway, but the crowd only moved to the top of Pier Road, overlooking the harbour. The old cries of 'one, two, three, four; who the hell are

we for?' were vociferously answered by 'Churchill!' 'England!' 'Jersey!'"

Diary of Leslie Sinel, September 18th 1942

Not everyone who had been told to report to the harbour had made it onto the boat. They were told it was full, and to go home and wait until the next one. Some returned to find their homes had already been looted. Most of them got their turn, as other boats left in the coming days.

In Guernsey, there were similar scenes, as islanders were taken from their homes at very short notice with no indication of where they would be going. Everywhere there were people saying goodbyes, with no idea of when, or if, they might see each other again.

Around 1,200 men, women and children were deported from Jersey, and another 800 from Guernsey.

Imagine being given just twelve hours notice to leave your home, for the unknown. What would you take with you? What would you leave behind? Who would you want to say goodbye to? And how would you explain it to your children?

THE CAMPS

The hundreds of deportees were in for a very long journey. Finally getting off the old boats in St Malo they were herded onto trains for a three day journey across France and into Germany. The lucky ones had managed to make provision for themselves. Michael Ginns' mother had been very pragmatic....

"I had a lovely pet rabbit, which I had named Sooty. The day the Germans knocked on our door, Sooty mysteriously disappeared. On the long train journey to Germany the mystery was explained, as we tucked into Sooty sandwiches."

Most of the deportees from Guernsey were taken to a camp in the town of Biberach, in the south west of Germany close to the border with France. While some of the men were sent to a camp at Laufen or other establishments, most Jersey families were crammed into an old castle in the centre of the small town of Wurzach, (later named Bad Wurzach).

More than six hundred Jersey folk spent the rest of the war behind the barbed wire and stone walls of the *schloss*. The rest were held in other locations across Germany. It is important to note that these were not in any way *concentration camps*. They didn't exist to punish or to kill people, there were no beatings and no forced labour.

But while they weren't harshly treated, the deportees were in cramped conditions with sometimes erratic food supplies. Michael Ginns remembered being allowed out of the camp to fetch bread for the internees from the town bakery. Any thought of escape would have been tempered by the view from the castle windows of the Hitler Youth training school in the fields immediately adjacent. Occasionally they were allowed outside the camp for walks – always escorted by armed guards....

> "It would have been difficult for any of us to run away; where were we going
> to run to? Eventually we got to know them so well, on the way back from the
> walks they would let us stop at the local pub and we would all pool our few
> pennies we were allowed, to buy the guard a beer."
>
> Juanita Shield-Laignel, *Occupation Reconciliation*,

For the children in particular it was a strange and unnatural existence, forced to sleep in dormitories with other families and denied the full education they would have received at home.

But as proud Jersey people they survived, making entertainments for themselves and gathering snippets of news as best they could from friendly guards. The summers were warm and stuffy for those cooped up inside, while the winters were freezing with snow covering the hills around and raising the risk of disease and hypothermia.

In all, forty four Channel Island deportees died while in enemy camps.

The rest finally came home late in the summer of 1945, after liberation and a sojourn in England. For some it was a joyous return; others found their houses ransacked or demolished, knocked down to build defences or to clear fields of fire.

Decades later, largely thanks to the efforts of Michael Ginns, there is a strong and thriving bond between Jersey and the town of Bad Wurzach. Former internees make regular trips to the castle, where they are met warmly by the townsfolk. The former mayor, Roland Bürkle, was involved in twinning the town with St Helier as part of a *Partnerschaft* agreement.

> "Forgiveness leads to understanding. Understanding leads to friendship.
> Friendship leads to reconciliation. Reconciliation leads to peace,
> both in our hearts and in the world."
>
> Michael Ginns MBE

Laufen, where some of the Jersey deportees were held

The castle at Wurzach where more than six hundred Jersey men, women and children spent three years imprisoned

Biberach Camp

Michael Ginns MBE with the Mayor of Bad Wurzach,
Roland Bürkle: a lasting friendship

6 RESISTANCE

"You couldn't take to the mountains in Jersey with arms in hand. First we've got
no mountains and second we've got no arms"

Norman Le Brocq

Many people ask "Where was the resistance in Jersey?"

In France, the exploits of the *Maquis* became a powerful national symbol of hope
during the years of occupation, as brave men and women blew up trains, killed
Germans and fought epic battles across mountain plateaus. After the war they
became an important symbol of pride for a country which found it hard to accept
that it had been beaten so easily when the Germans invaded.

In Jersey though there was no shooting, no dramatic nighttime landing of arms
supplies, no bands of armed men hiding in caves to pounce on German convoys.
Such things were simply not feasible in a place as remote and densely populated....

"Any kind of real resistance was simply impossible in an island where one
in every five people was a German and there was no chance of getting an
arms drop or support from the mainland. Even if there had been, any kind of
collective action.... would have been utterly futile in such a small island where
there was nowhere to hide, prepare or train."

Bob Le Sueur, *Growing Up Fast*

Recently opened documents from the archive show that more than five hundred
Jersey people were arrested and punished by the Germans for 'political crimes'.
These could range from spreading the BBC news to stealing weapons or trying
to escape.

THE 'V' SIGN

In the early days their weapons of choice were brushes and tins of paint. Defying
the curfew, individuals would daub 'V' for victory in prominent places, often over
German signs, where they would be sure to see them. They had the idea from
Winston Churchill himself, who famously raised his fingers in a 'V', and the BBC

ATTENTION—WARNING

Any persons found marking walls
with 'V' signs or insults against
the German Armed Forces
are liable to be shot.

A reward will be paid
to any persons giving information
that will lead to the arrest
of these offenders.

G. V. Schmettow
General,
German Military Government

Don Le Gallais, who made illegal crystal radio sets

which used the morse side for 'V' to introduce its news bulletins.

The Germans were of course angry at such blatant signs of opposition, and took action.

Anyone caught risked severe treatment at the hands of the German Field Police, who investigated any incidents they found. Edward Le Quesne was less than impressed with the campaign....

> "Another of those silly incidents which jeopardise our liberties occurred today. Someone.... took it on themselves to write in paint on the walls of the German headquarters "Britain's Victory is Certain" and all over the town huge 'V's have been painted. Whether we agree with the sentiments expressed is besides the point. The facts are that Jerry is furious.... a great deal of harm is done by this silly type of patriotism."
>
> *Diary of Edward Le Quesne,* 29 June 1941

One of the people to be arrested was Joe Mière, the future manager of the Jersey War Tunnels. He was taken to Silvertide, the building on the east coast which was the headquarters of the German Secret Field Police – the closest the island had to the dreaded *Gestapo*....

> "as soon as you got in the door you had a fist in the face and another in the stomach. Before you know where you are you're on the floor spitting blood. You look back on things like that and say – that's life."

Contrary to popular belief, the dreaded secret state police or *Gestapo* never operated in Jersey. Instead, the Secret Field Police (*Geheimefeldpolizei*) carried out investigations into any suspected resistance activity. Its officers wore the long black leather coats and slouched hats made notorious by the *Gestapo*, and used similarly intimidating methods in their inquiries.

Despite the risks, the 'V' campaign was something everyone could join in. Soon, it appeared in patterns on peoples clothing, on decorations in peoples homes, and thanks to the artist Edmund Blampied, on the new editions of Jersey stamps. Held upside down, the 'V' was clear to those who knew where to look!

Some 'V' signs were even more creative – and more permanent. If you visit the Royal Square in St Helier, look closely at the granite paving and you'll notice there is a large 'V' set into the stones. It was put there by stonemason Joe Le Guyadier who worked in the square during the Occupation, and fortunately the Germans failed to notice it while it boosted the morale of all the islanders who walked there.

It wasn't Joe's first act of defiance. When the Germans were forced to scuttle the battleship Graf Spee at the end of 1939, he was working on the granite cladding of the Church of the Sacred Heart in St Aubin. In celebration of the naval victory he incorporated a small anchor in the designs above the doorway.

Despite threats of punishment the Germans eventually realised there would be no easy way to force people to abandon the 'V' campaign – so they found an ingenious solution. They adapted it for themselves. Soon the 'V' was part of many designs for German signposts and insignia, and lost some of its appeal for the islanders who had used it as their own symbol of opposition and hope.

While many islanders were prepared to join the 'V' campaign, there were others who tried to take more active measures against their occupiers. The Germans had of course taken over the island's telephone network, and laid many extra lines themselves to join their various bunkers and command positions. They were a tempting target for young men keen to make an impression.

Pam Le Cornu's father Reg Robins was one of them, and he cut some wires with a group of his friends. It wasn't long before he was identified and taken down to the dreaded Silvertide. They took his identity card and made it clear that he would be tried and possibly sent away to prison in occupied Europe. Pam remembers how they saved him from what could have been a dreadful fate....

"My mother knew of a Jerrybag who lived down the road, who she never spoke to because of her lifestyle. She went there on her hands and knees and sure enough this girl spoke to the officer she was courting who worked at Silvertide. But the officer wasn't going to let him get away with it scot-free. So he sentenced him to two weeks guarding the telephone lines that he'd already cut!"

It was a lucky escape for Reg. If the Germans had searched his house more thoroughly they may have found the equipment that he used to make crystal radio sets for his friends and neighbours....

LISTENING IN THE DARK – LONDON CALLING

1942 was a turning point in the Occupation of Jersey. Until then, the Germans had treated islanders with respect and there had been no particularly harsh measures directed against them. But in that year, three things happened to change the atmosphere entirely; the deportation of hundreds of non-native islanders to captivity in Germany, the arrival of the slaves; and the ban on owning a radio.

For many this was the most oppressive measure yet. Jersey people relied on the BBC to keep them informed of what was happening in the outside world; without it they would feel even more cut off and isolated than ever before. They were faced with a simple choice – should they do as they were told, surrender their radio, and live without that reassuring link with freedom? Or should they defy the order and run the risk of discovery and an unknown punishment?

For thousands the choice was simple, and they found ingenious ways to hide their wireless sets. Some were hidden under floorboards, in chicken coops, old barrels or secret compartments in book cases. Across the island, families, friends and brave individuals hid in the dark to hear the voice of freedom from across the sea.

Dr John Lewis, who'd stayed in the island because he felt it was his duty to look after his patients, couldn't bear to be without the BBC....

> "I took some bricks out from the side of my chimney in the drawing room and concealed the wireless set in the wall.... it was essential to me to have the news and hear what was going on in England and elsewhere. The Germans never found it."

Doreen Hills' parents were the caretakers of the Wesley Chapel. They hid their radio under the organ, which a German officer used to play once a week....

> "I never saw him but my mother did. There was a funeral one Thursday afternoon and she was just coming through the vestry after closing the church when she saw this German officer. He smiled and went out although he came again many times, week after week, he never realised that he was sitting on top of a wireless set."

Donald Le Gallais was one of the many who knew how to make 'crystal' wireless sets, which were tiny and more easily concealed. He made them for people he knew, and was at a farmhouse one day testing a set when a German marched unexpectedly in. (Many islanders remember that officers didn't bother to wait for an invitation, but simply came straight in through the door.)

The officer pushed a pistol into his back and demanded to know what he was doing. When Don confessed, the officer immediately relaxed....

> "He wasn't the Nazi type and he knew the Germans couldn't win the war. He told the farmer that he wouldn't say anything about the wireless because he was going to come back from time to time to listen to the English news. In the end he was giving us sets of headphones."

It's perhaps easy to forget that the Jersey people weren't the only ones starved of real news. The average German soldier was fed nothing but propaganda, and was kept in the dark about the real progress of the war and the bombing back at home. For many of them, getting illicit BBC news from islanders was the one way they could stay informed.

But it was still a very risky business. Possessing a radio, listening to it, and sharing what you heard, was punishable by strong sentences, and it cost some their lives. No-one was exempt, as the states Deputy and diarist Edward Le Quesne found out on 9 September 1944. He was arrested after German police searched his home and found his wireless which he had hidden 'behind a fowl house'. Baron von Aufsess pleaded his case in court, but nonethless he was sentenced to seven months in prison.

> "Asked to state from whom I had bought the set, I asked 'Do you think I would descend so low as to turn informer?' The judge answered <u>NO</u> and shook hands with me."
>
> *Diary of Edward Le Quesne,* 26 September 1944.

He only served part of his sentence, and was released on 23rd October.

Where would you hide a wireless set in your house so it would escape detection but still be easy to use?

CANON COHU: NO MERCY FOR THE CLERGY

Canon Clifford Cohu was fifty seven years old when the Germans invaded. Originally from Guernsey, he had come to the larger island to retire in 1937. He's remembered as a thoughtful and sensitive man, who could not bear the thought of freedom being oppressed. He was part of a ring of islanders who listened to the BBC news and then disseminated it between themselves on sheets of paper. Despite the risk he shared it with as many other people as possible through his job as Chaplain at the General Hospital and was even known to shout the latest news out loud as he rode his bike along busy streets.

It couldn't last, and together with other members of his circle he was arrested and tried. There was rarely any doubt about the outcome of such a process, and they were all sentenced to prison terms on the continent. After a long and difficult journey through various prisons and camps, he ended up in Zöschen, a forced labour camp. Already weak from disease, starvation and maltreatment, it's believed this gentle man was beaten to death by one of the notoriously brutal camp guards. As they prepared his body for burial, they found a bible clutched to his chest.

Despite the risks, many Jersey people kept their radios throughout the Occupation and heard news which became more and more encouraging as it went on. Bob Le Sueur was at a friend's house when he heard of the capitulation of Italy in 1943. Flushed with excitement, they went out into the streets of St Helier, to find that others were doing exactly the same. By some hidden telepathy, everyone headed to the Royal Square....

> "We all had the swing of elation in our walks. The Germans who saw us knew why we suddenly seemed so pleased. And they knew that we knew that they knew why – and still nobody said a thing. In very friendly terms we greeted relative strangers as though they were long lost friends.... it was a wonderful demonstration of shared spirit and unity. Whenever any news of that kind came out it was all over the island in an hour."
>
> Bob Le Sueur, *Growing Up Fast*

But perhaps the most beloved announcement of all came on May 8th 1945. In the same Royal Square where they had furtively celebrated the fall of Italy, on the flagstones inscribed with the hidden 'V' sign, thousands of islanders gathered to listen to speakers rigged up on trees with the agreement of the Germans. The voice of Sir Winston Churchill boomed out to huge cheers....

> ".... and our dear Channel Islands are to be FREED...."

The Bailiff suggested that anyone who had managed to hide a radio for the past three years would face no action if they switched it on that day. Bob Le Sueur and his family had never revealed to anyone that they had kept theirs, hidden in a pile of old clothes behind a living room chair. They got it out and put it on full volume on the windowsill, only to discover that their neighbours on both sides had done exactly the same!

OUR FELLOW MAN – THE PLIGHT OF THE SLAVES

> "An incident of gross cruelty was witnessed today and has shocked the island and brought home to many people who up till now had suggested that the Germans were not as bad as they have been painted, how inhuman the enemy can be in his treatment of helpless and defenceless prisoners. Some 1100 prisoners from the Ukraine arrived in the early morning. A large number were mere boys of between fourteen and sixteen years of age. Others were men of seventy and over, and hardly any were men who looked anything like soldiers. Few had boots or shoes, some had no coats and some had only a ladies blouse and a pair of trousers.

All looked half starved and were in the charge of fat bellied Organisation Todt men armed with rubber truncheons and whips.

Women cried to see the pitiful sight and one bus load stopped and the passengers offered their seats to some of the poor wretches who looked in a dying condition. This help was brutally refused by the Germans. This incident has caused a tremendous sensation amongst local people and expressions of indignation can be heard on all sides."

Diary of Edward Le Quesne, 13 August 1942.

For many Jersey people this represented an important change in how they perceived the regime that controlled them. For two years the Germans had been at pains to show that they were polite, reasonable and fair, keen to carry out what the author Madeleine Bunting described as a 'Model Occupation'. But when this desperate, pitiful group arrived the islanders attitude altered as they recognised the true nature of the Nazi empire.

The confiscation of their radios and the deportation of hundreds of non-native people in the same year only accelerated that process.

This prosperous British island had never seen this kind of brutality, and it prompted many who had until then been happy simply to endure the Occupation to take action. As the poor, starving wretches foraged for food and warmth they found help from people ready to take pity on them....

"I have felt so sad in thinking of these poor men. They looked so dreadfully tired and sad, so far from home, and one is constantly hearing of the bestial way in which the Germans treat them, beating them even to death."

Diary of Nan Le Ruez, 14 September 1942

The forced workers and slaves existed on a diet far too low in calories and nutrients to sustain life – especially when considering how hard they had to work. To sustain them for a twelve hour day of intense labour and abuse, their allocated ration was: a cup of black 'coffee' for breakfast, some thin vegetable soup for lunch, and more soup in the evening together with 200g of bread. Sometimes they would get a smear of butter, or piece of sausage. Those rations were often fought over, especially the bread when a one kilo loaf was shared between five men. Starvation led to some slaves breaking out of their camps and begging or stealing from local people.

Some islanders, especially those who lived in the countryside, were able to shelter escaped slaves in their barns, or even just leave food out for them. It was dangerous though, as the Germans were liable to appear in force without warning.

Alan Rabet's parents were farmers who helped a handful of runaways. One day they heard a large German patrol marching down the lane towards the farmhouse....

"We had managed to push them out of the back window. We were lined up in the kitchen at gunpoint and this German was yelling 'Russki soldaten, Russki soldaten!'"

Luckily the slaves had managed to escape across a waterlogged meadow and the family avoided any punishment.

Other islanders took escaped workers into their homes, and treated them as their own. Phyllis Le Breton was a farmers wife in St Mary....

"I was in the kitchen when he tapped on the window.... the children loved him and when he could understand some English he used to read them fairy stories."

Official German figures show that seventy three Russian or Ukranian workers died in the island during the Occupation, together with forty eight from other countries. They are buried in the Strangers Cemetery at Westmount, where there is a memorial service for them every year.

Several of the escapees are thought to have worked at Ho8. In August 1944, at least five were listed as missing from the employ of contractors Karl Plötner, who were running excavation work there.

Not everyone who helped was lucky enough to get away with it. One of the most notorious stories of the Occupation, which has been the subject of a major film, saw a middle aged Jersey woman die at Ravensbrück because she wanted to help 'Another Mother's Son'.

THE ULTIMATE SACRIFICE – LOUISA GOULD AND RUSSIAN BILL

Feodor Polycarpovitch Burriy was a Russian serviceman who was captured in one of the early German advances across his country in 1941. Herded into railway trucks with thousands of his fellow countrymen, he was brought west to help the German war effort in occupied Europe. He ended up on a packed and dirty boat which took him to Jersey.

He was sent to work at the stone crushing plant at the bottom of the hill which

Louisa Gould sacrificed her life to save 'Russian Bill'

Bill with Bob Le Sueur after Liberation

leads from St Ouen's Village to the Five Mile Road, known as Mont Pinel. Life there was made very hard by aggressive O.T. overseers, who would beat any man who they considered to be slacking. Unable to endure the treatment, and desperately hungry, he tried to escape only to be quickly recaptured. He was beaten mercilessly while being forced to push a wheelbarrow full of stones around the courtyard, until he collapsed. Then he was made to stand in a barrel full of cold water through the long autumn night.

He survived – and incredibly decided to try again. With the help of fellow slaves who created a diversion, he climbed over the wall and tried to get away. Luckily for him a Jersey farmer was coming down the hill in a vehicle powered by a large gas bag on the roof. He stopped and beckoned the terrified slave inside. Off they went, and the farmer dropped the runaway at the bottom of a hill further down the road. He scrambled upwards through bushes and gorse before trying to get into a small shed in the corner of a farmer's field – only to be grabbed and attacked by another slave who was already hiding inside!

The farm was owned by René Le Mottée, who had already sheltered several slaves who had managed to escape. This brave man had a series of friends who would take them on when he accumulated too many.

One of those was a middle-aged widow called Louisa Gould who ran a small shop next door to her house, which was close to René's farm. She took in this latest escaper – and re-christened him Bill. She told people:

"I had to do something for another mother's son."

She had lost her only son who died fighting with the Royal Navy, and Bill soon became a way for her to overcome her grief. She fed and clothed him, and even allowed him to work in her shop where he was seen by many local people, passing himself off as French. He studied English, and went with Mrs Gould to church.

It was at the shop where Bob Le Sueur first met him.

"I knew enough French and French people to recognise a genuine Gallic accent, and this was most certainly not one. I presumed straight away that he was an escaped Russian slave."

Bob Le Sueur, *Growing Up Fast*

Although he was appalled at first by Louisa Gould's indiscretion, Bob quickly made friends with Bill, and was even able to get a doctored identity card for him so that he could draw rations. Bill became part of a social group, and was taken to visit trusted friends.

Inevitably though his identity was discovered and Mrs Gould received warnings

Louisa Gould and her sons in happier times

In This House
Mrs Louisa Mary Gould,
née Le Druillenec,
Sheltered An Escaped Russian P.O.W.
During The German Occupation
From October 1942 Until May 1944.
After Her Arrest She Was
Deported To The Concentration
Camp At Ravensbruck
Where She Perished
In The Gas Chamber.

from two sources that the game was up. Hastily destroying any evidence of Bill's existence, she moved him into town to stay with her brother and sister, Ivy Forster and Harold Le Druillenec. But she hadn't been thorough enough, and when the German police arrived they found a Russian-English dictionary and other items which made it clear that Mrs Gould had been sheltering a wanted man. As she was taken to prison, Bob Le Sueur spirited Bill away, installing him in a series of homes for the rest of the war. They were never caught, and celebrated Liberation together. His final hosts, for several months, were two conscientious objectors who had come to Jersey to escape the threat of war in 1939. Mike Frowd and René Franoux would never have fired a gun in anger, yet they endured the long drawn-out fear of harbouring a wanted man, knowing they could be discovered at any moment. Bravery is not only found on the battlefield.

For Louisa and her family the outcome was far worse. They were all sentenced to prison and taken away from the island. Ivy Forster managed to escape when their prison in Rennes was bombed, and she was rescued by the advancing Americans soon afterwards.

Harold was beaten and abused through the German penal system until he ended up in Belsen concentration camp. He is thought to be the only British survivor of that awful place, and went on to give evidence about what had happened there to war crimes investigators after being freed in extremely bad health.

Louisa became one of the twenty one islanders commemorated on the Lighthouse Memorial to those who died in German prisons during the war. Transported to the notorious Ravensbrück concentration camp, she was killed in February 1945. Her name is also on the St Ouen parish war memorial close to her home.

"I was enormously sad that such a heroic, warm hearted and loving woman could have met such a wretched end. In doing something for another mother's son, she paid with her life."

Bob Le Sueur, *Growing Up Fast*

REVOLUTIONARIES: THE JERSEY COMMUNIST PARTY

Norman Le Brocq was a young and idealistic communist who was appalled when his island was invaded by the Nazis. He set about recruiting a small group of like-minded friends who could offer some kind of organised resistance to the new regime.

As well as helping to move and hide escaped slaves, Norman and his group ran a very risky but effective campaign of subversion against their enemies, and even plotted to incite disillusioned Germans troops to mutiny as the end drew close.

With the help of Spanish-speaking friends, they wrote leaflets urging Spanish workers in the island to revolt against their masters, and had them clandestinely printed and distributed. When the Ukranian and Russian slaves arrived, they managed to get similar documents printed in Russian, and shared out around the camps.

But possibly the most dangerous venture was an attempt to get German soldiers themselves to turn against their own leaders. In this, they were helped and encouraged by a deserter named Paul Mühlbach, whose father had been killed in a concentration camp and was set on revenge against the Nazis who had put him there. Mühlbach was hidden in a house near the Longueville Manor Hotel, where he sat in darkness with the curtains drawn writing new pamphlets urging his fellow soldiers to revolt. Bob Le Sueur was taken there to be recruited into the group. After a clandestine night-time rendezvous half a mile away, he followed Norman Le Brocq at a distance on his bicycle. They stopped at the cottage where Mühlbach was hiding, and were allowed in after whistling some bars of *Eine Kleine Nachtmusik* by way of coded greeting.

> "As he closed the door softly, I heard a whistling sound from upstairs. Mozart again! We followed the sound upstairs in the dark , and Norman pushed open a door. A man sat at a typewriter on a desk, dimly lit by an oil light. He wore a splendid blue suit and badly dyed blonde hair."
>
> Bob Le Sueur, *Growing Up Fast*

Paul Mühlbach became the inspiration for the group's activities, at great risk to all concerned. Making extensive use of their secret copying machine, in the spring of 1945 they began to circulate leaflets to German soldiers telling them that the war was lost, that Germany was in flames, and that that their destiny lay in their own hands. By way of example, Mühlbach had already destroyed a German garage and storage shed. But his most notable achievement was when, in his soldier's uniform, he set fire to the Palace Hotel in St Saviour which was being used as a German headquarters. The resulting explosions, some of which were probably caused by soldiers trying to block the progress of the fire, destroyed the building entirely and cost nine German lives.

The climax to these acts of insurrection was to have come on 1 May 1945. While the war was all but won, there was no indication that Jersey would be freed any time soon. *Vizeadmiral* Friedrich Hüffmeier, a fervent Nazi, was now in command of the island and had told his troops there would be no surrender without a fight. Paul Mühlbach, with help from the Jersey Communists, managed to contact and

Comrades,

In Germany at this time the collapse of the Hitler regime is reaching completion. The Nazis are trying, with bloody proclamations to summon even the women and children to resistance against the allies. But the German people will no longer tolerate this swindle and now the Nazi blackguards are forced to defend their lives themselves after having hunted millions to death for the mad ideas of a Hitler.

Soldiers of the Channel Islands. Decide now your fate for yourselves. Keep your weapons ready for the settlement with the lawless Nazi officers and their cronies.

Note the following:- When the signal for the uprising comes, bind a white cloth or a handkerchief around the left arm, otherwise follow the orders of your representatives. All officers are to be arrested as a matter of principle, and in case of resistance to be shot. Under-officers and men, who give themselves out to be Nazis are to be similarly treated. Such officers as belong to the resistance movement will, at the appropriate time, stand at your side with advice and action.

UNDEROFFICERS: Cease to follow the false teachings of your officers, rely more on your natural, healthy common-sense, have confidence in the men. Stand together, and help in the disposal of the Nazis otherwise you share their responsibility, in such a case your fate will be that of all war criminals.

SOLDIERS: Don't shoot at saboteurs, even in the case of persons in civilian clothes. Consider that every dead Nazi, every blown up munitions dump, every burnt out officers' quarters helps YOU

Think of your future, save yourselves by one great, liberating deed.

Down with the Nazi slavery.

All for Germany.

Anti-Nazi propaganda produced by the deserter Paul Mühlbach

persuade some troops to mutiny at ten o'clock that morning. The signal would be the firing of a cannon from the ramparts of Elizabeth Castle. While this was an enormous risk to all concerned, the Communists had their eyes on a bigger prize; with the Germans defeated, there would be a moment of opportunity for them to take over the island's government in a *coup d'état*.

Perhaps fortunately for all sides on that cold Spring morning the cannon never fired, and the 'revolution' fizzled out. Bob Le Sueur, who had been waiting nervously for the signal at First Tower, was relieved that bloodshed had been avoided. The revolution, he said, had melted away like the snow on the pavement. Jersey was liberated peacefully nine days later.

GETTING OFF THE ROCK – THE ESCAPES

Jersey has a proud seafaring history, and many young men in particular hoped they could escape the occupation of their island by sailing away from it. Some were successful, some failed; some ended in tragedy.

Denis Vibert was twenty one when he made his first attempt to get away, setting out from the east of the island in a rowing boat one November night in 1944. Problems with currents left him stranded on some rocks near Guernsey, but he managed to get back to Jersey albeit suffering from influenza and exposure.

His next attempt a year later was a success. Despite his outboard motor failing, and his spare motor falling into the sea, Denis managed to row with the tides until he was picked up by a Royal Navy ship and taken to safety. Unbelievably British Customs charged him ten shillings import duty for his boat!

After the invasion of Normandy in 1944 the Cherbourg peninsula was liberated by the Allies. Its low coastline is easily visible from Jersey's east coast, and many more young Jersey men decided to risk the crossing. With the help of local people such as the Bertrams at Fauvic, they rowed and sailed their way across the dangerous fifteen mile stretch of water. It has one of the highest tidal ranges in the world, and is treacherous to those without luck or skill.

Three young men had a catastrophic crossing, and two of them paid with their lives. Peter Hassall, Dennis Audrain and Maurice Gould got just two miles off shore when their boat sank beneath them. Dennis couldn't swim and drowned in the rough sea while his companions managed to swim back to land. Unfortunately for them the Germans were waiting, and both were arrested and thrown into prison after a search revealed they had information about the occupying forces with them. Deported to France, they became victims of the Nazi penal system. Maurice died of

A suuccessful escaper: Denis Vibert ...

... and one who perished: Maurice Gould

TB after being badly treated, while Peter was sent to a Polish coal mine. Of the three brave escapers, he was the only one to survive the war.

Fifty nine people escaped from Jersey. Six were drowned, and another six were recaptured to be killed or imprisoned by the Germans. Forty seven made it to safety.

One of those who made it was the young Peter Crill, who would one day be knighted as Jersey's Bailiff. He was lucky to make it that far, because after battling through dangerous seas and jagged rocks, he nearly lost his life on the beach where he landed....

"At the place where we came ashore there wasn't anyone in sight. So we dragged the boat up and went on to find a local bistro. Inside one of the men said – which way did you come? We pointed to where we had left tracks in the sand. And they said – you're very lucky because that part of the beach hasn't been cleared yet of mines."

Would you have risked your life – and the lives of your family – to help an escaped prisoner? Would you have cut phone wires or daubed 'V' signs on German walls? Would you have been brave enough to slip seditious messages into the pockets of German soldiers? Or even harbour a deserter?

MORT POUR LA PATRIE – THE STORY OF FRANÇOIS SCORNET

After the fall of France, many young French men heard the call to arms broadcast by Charles de Gaulle – which some believe was written during his flight to England via Jersey. They determined to try to answer. François Scornet was one of them, and with a group of sixteen friends decided to sail from their home in Brittany across the Channel to England.

Navigational problems saw them taken off course though, and they landed on a beach in Guernsey. Believing they had landed on the Isle of Wight, they waded ashore singing *La Marseillaise*, only to be arrested by bemused German guards. They were all taken to Jersey and tried before a German court in the first case of its kind, held in a room in the states building. Most were sentenced to prison, possibly because this was early in the Occupation and the Germans were still trying to keep relations with the islanders calm.

Scornet though was identified as the ringleader and condemned to death.

BEKANNTMACHUNG:

FRANÇOIS SCORNET,

geb. 25·5  ohnhaft in

Ploujean (Istere) ist

wegen Be ndes durch

beabsichti Englands

im Kriege sche Reich

du icht

ZUM TODE

verurteilt und am 17·III·1941

erschossen worden.

Das Kriegsgericht.

Den 23·III·1941.

PUBLICATION:

The population is herewith notified, that
FRANÇOIS SCORNET,
born on May 25th 1919, residing in
Plouiean (Department: Finistere) has
been sentenced

TO DEATH

by the German War Court and has
been shot on March 17th, 1941. This
had to be done, because of his favouring
the actions of the enemy by wilfully
supporting England in the war against
the German Empire.

German War Court.
March 23rd, 1941.

Held at the Grand Hotel while preparations were made, he was finally taken to his execution on 17 March 1941. He was driven in a lorry sitting on his own coffin to the grounds of St Ouen's Manor, where he was shot by a twelve man firing squad. His final words were "*Vive la France!*"

"I PROTESTED" – THE ROLE OF THE AUTHORITIES

Since the war ended there has been long debate about the role played by the island authorities during the Occupation. Some argue that they did their best under very difficult circumstances; while others claim they were complicit in allowing the Germans to deport people and persecute the Jews.

The Bailiff, Alexander Coutanche, was in the difficult position of trying to act as a buffer between the German military rulers and the people of the island. As such he was forced into many compromises, which would never be popular with everyone but were perhaps the best way to keep as many people safe for as long as possible. He and other island representatives thought it would be fruitless to fight battles they knew they could not win and risk being bypassed completely leaving the islanders with no protection. Their aim was to soften the blows aimed at the island by Berlin.

For example, when in October 1940 the Germans demanded that they identify Jewish people living in the island they unwillingly agreed to help, and Jews had their status clearly marked on their identification papers. But when Berlin demanded that they should also be forced to wear the Yellow Star, Coutanche argued strongly against the order – and was successful.

There were more covert ways in which they could help. A German order forbade Jews from running businesses, and instructed that all such concerns should be sold. With the collusion of the authorities, several were 'bought' for a minimal sum, on the understanding that they could be exchanged once more after the war for the same amount.

Some Jews were allowed to live freely without being subject to other constraints, for example the eccentric artist Claude Cahun and her lover Marcel Moore (real names Lucie Schwob and Suzanne Malherbe) who lived in St Brelade's Bay. Not only did they continue their lives as normal but they risked their lives to distribute anti-Nazi propaganda and BBC news reports among German soldiers. Often they would slip them into soldier's pockets or throw them through open car windows, until they were finally caught in July 1944.

They were sentenced to death, but the Bailiff intervened. In a letter to the *Platzcommandant*, Coutanche said that the sentence was causing 'anxiety and distress' among islanders, and that he wanted to avoid anything that caused 'passion' among the population. He appealed for mercy; and the women's sentence was commuted to prison.

It wasn't the only time he was successful in changing a death sentence. Incidents like these pose the question; if Alexander Coutanche had simply defied the Germans on all counts, as some believe he should have, would he have been in any position to influence decisions such as these?

He was also aware of at least one escape from the island. In August 1944 Jersey was cut off from France as the Allies occupied Normandy and the Cherbourg Peninsula. Coutanche had his officers draw up an appraisal of the food stocks left in the island, and how long they might be able to last. The answer was pessimistic. He passed the details to the Germans who had agreed to forward them to the Red Cross, but wasn't convinced it would be of any use. Consequently, he passed the report on to a young man called Norman Rumboll, who he knew was planning to make an escape. In doing so, he was putting himself at great risk, because if Rumboll had been caught with the documents there would be little doubt where he had got them from.

After the war, the author Charles Cruikshank considered what role the island authorities under the Bailiff had played. He recognised that they had been in a very difficult position, but had come out of it as well as possible....

"…. they carried the administrative war to the enemy camp on many occasions. It is not that they made some mistakes that is surprising, but that they did so much right in circumstances of the greatest possible difficulty."
Charles Cruikshank, *The German Occupation of the Channel Islands*

Alexander Coutanche was knighted in 1946 for leading the island through the Occupation. The title was not approved of by some, including the Communist leader Norman Le Brocq who felt the Bailiff had failed to protect the Jews and other vulnerable groups.

Coutanche knew all too well that his actions during the war would always be a source of fierce debate. But he believed that he had succeeded in walking that very fine line between protecting his people and inciting more oppressive measures from the Germans....

"When asked by my grandchildren what I did during the Occupation I shall say, 'I protested'"

7 COLLABORATION AND FRATERNISATION

> "I believe the pejorative term 'collaboration' can often be confused with
> the less serious charge of 'fraternisation'. There is an important difference.
> To me, collaboration is actively seeking to help the enemy to win the war.
> Fraternisation is informal contact with other individuals who happen to be
> wearing a different kind of clothing.... I am sure that most of us had a
> moment in the Occupation when we thought 'not all Germans are bad.'"
> Bob Le Sueur, *Growing Up Fast*

> "Whether he wants blonde or brunette, married or single, fat or thin,
> young or old – Jerry can always get a good selection."
> *Diary of Philip Le Sauteur*, 31 July 1940

The question of whether Jersey people *collaborated* with their occupiers is fraught with complexities. Some, most recently the historian Madeleine Bunting, argue that the people and the authorities were largely complacent and allowed the Germans to take over and dominate the island without much of a fight. Others point to myriad acts of brave subterfuge and deception which defied the regime and sustained the island's pride. As with so many of these questions, the true picture is somewhere between these two extremes.

It is a fact that many Jersey people willingly denounced their fellow islanders, in return for favours, money, or simply for petty revenge.

It is a fact that there were no great acts of sabotage as there were in France and other occupied countries; no trains derailed, no armed uprisings, no Generals kidnapped or factories destroyed.

It is a fact that many islanders worked for the Germans voluntarily, in return for payment.

It is a fact that some Jersey women became the lovers of German soldiers.

But it is also a fact that every year there is a memorial service to twenty one islanders who were killed in German camps for having broken the military laws by spreading the BBC news, trying to escape, or in one case slapping a German officer who made improper advances.

It is also a fact that many Ukranian and Russian slave workers were saved from death by the bravery of ordinary people who often went unheralded. They fed them, hid them, and risked their lives to save them from the search teams who raided homes with machine guns.

Jersey people also sheltered, clothed and fed escaped American POWs and helped them to steal a boat and return to France.

And it is a fact that thousands of islanders defied the German ruling that all radios should be surrendered to prevent anyone from tuning in to 'enemy' stations. All over Jersey behind closed curtains or in hidden attic rooms people gathered to listen very quietly to clandestine receivers and then share the news discreetly with friends and family.

Secrecy was paramount. It was not until years after the war that Bob Le Sueur discovered that his reserved and shy secretary had smuggled letters and documents into the American POW camp at Mount Bingham in the handlebars of her bicycle. She, like many others, had quietly risked everything without telling a soul.

Women who enjoyed the company of German soldiers or officers were known as *Jerrybags*.

JERRYBAGS

When Jersey was invaded in 1940 thousands of her young men were missing, having evacuated or joined the armed forces. The Germans who arrived were fit, young, polite and smart in new, well cut uniforms. It was part of a deliberate attempt to seduce the island, to reassure everyone that occupation by the German soldier was not a thing to be feared.

The inevitable result was that some young women – and some older ones – fell for their charms. It happened quickly; Philip Le Sauteur noted just two weeks after the Occupation began….

"I have been amazed at how calmly people have taken this Occupation – all except the younger female section who are thrilled to bits. It is blasted shameful to see brats of 15 and 16, as well as older (and who should be more sensible) females offering themselves to German soldiers. And there is more than one British soldier's wife going out to dances with them"

Diary of Philip Le Sauteur, 15 July 1940

"On the beach complete amity still reigns between the German soldiers and local girls. With a few exceptions the girl will surrender to her partner readily

All the same with our uniforms off….?

Soldiers and local women relax in the sun together

One of many letters of denunciation. Note the stamps; can you spot the hidden 'V'?

Why is Jack Le Cornu, 4 Doyne Terrace, Great Union Road, allowed to have received 1 ton of Anthracite Coal when other people have none at all.

Also call and see his stock of food in bedroom cupboards, and billiard room and see what you think of it ???

enough, provided this can be affected in proper privacy. The English woman is astoundingly simple, effortless and swift in her lovemaking."

Occupation Diary of Baron Von Aufsess

Some professed love, and quite possibly meant it, as in the example of Alice Thaureaux who was only fifteen when the war began and later fell for the handsome Nickolaus Schmitz. Theirs was a doomed love, which ended when he was shot for desertion shortly before liberation.

Others of course enjoyed the material benefits that being the lover of a soldier – ideally an officer – could bring.

Marjorie Robbins and her daughter Joan were well-known Jerrybag collaborators who lived on Midvale Road in St Helier. They welcomed the Germans with open arms and flaunted their relationships with high ranking officers. They even gave Nazi salutes to soldiers in the street, and held big noisy parties for them in their home. They made no secret of their attachments, which eventually proved their undoing.

INFORMERS

For anyone with a grudge against their neighbour, the Occupation was a convenient way to settle old scores. As the months passed, a steady stream of hand-written letters began to appear at the German headquarters at Victoria College House. They suggested that soldiers might like to search Mr X's chicken coop, or Miss Y's kitchen cupboards, whether for contraband food, cigarettes – or, even worse, hidden radios or escaped slaves. The Germans were happy to act on such information, and even offered a reward to anyone who supplied it. Not all of them were motivated by vengeance or greed. Some were simply starving, or needed the money to buy clothes for their children or food for ailing parents, others were simply jealous that their neighbours had something that they didn't.

> You could receive up to a hundred pounds for successfully denouncing an offender to the Germans. You would have to sign a receipt to say you had received it though, which led to some informers being identified after the war.

Some letters could be intercepted, and there's no doubt that the headmaster of Victoria College saved some islanders from arrest and even death. Informants weren't always clear about the difference between Victoria College, which continued as an educational establishment, and Victoria College House which was

Alexandrienne Baudains even wore a German uniform to flirt
with enemy soldiers. She was deported after the war

a German headquarters. The school secretary would often take delivery of letters from informers which had been incorrectly addressed, and pass them on to the headmaster, 'Pat' Tatum. He would steam them open, discover who was at risk, and then find a way to warn them that they were under suspicion and to get rid of whatever, or whoever, they were concealing. After a couple of days he would then re–seal the envelope with its letter inside, and forward it marked 'Wrong address – try Vic. Coll. House'. It was his intervention which is thought to have saved Louisa Gould from an early arrest, when she was denounced for hiding the slave known as 'Russian Bill'.

It is believed that Louisa was informed on by two sisters, Maud and Lily Vibert, who lived near Louisa and were thought to be jealous of her prosperous little shop. Their writing on the denunciation letter matched the document which confirmed they had received their reward money.

Thanks to the timely warning, Louisa managed to get Bill out of her house and into hiding with others, but the Germans still found enough evidence to put her on trial – and eventually kill her at Ravensbrück.

Perhaps the most infamous collaborator and 'Jerrybag' was Alexandrienne Baudains, known to most as 'Ginger Lou' or 'Mother Baudains'. She and her son were known to be ruthless in denouncing anyone who slighted or offended them in any way, and they became figures of island hatred and distrust. Her position was safe because she was the mistress of a high ranking officer which allowed her to treat her fellow islanders with contempt. Many of the people locked up in the town prison were there because of her.

Her experience of Liberation Day was very different to other islanders'. As a mob of angry people attacked their home, she and her son fled to the prison to ask for protection. There they stayed for eleven months, in the very place where she had caused so many of her fellow islanders to be incarcerated, until an article in the local newspaper blew their cover. Amid great outcry, the two were ignominiously deported and told never to return.

A similar fate befell Marjorie and Joan Robbins. After the Liberation, a mob dragged them from their home and was preparing to lynch them from a lamp post until a squad of soldiers saved them. After spending a time in prison for their own safety they too were deported.

While it's tempting to believe that the great bunkers and tunnels in Jersey were built exclusively by slave labour, it should be remembered that many Jersey men – and women – worked for their occupiers. The Germans were in need of skilled builders, drivers, secretaries and mechanics, specialised jobs which they could not always furnish themselves. Advertisements duly appeared in the *Evening Post*, offering higher rates of pay than usual to anyone willing to come to work on defence projects.

The motive of most of those who took the German *'mark'* was nearly always financial. At a time when wages in the island were capped at £3 a week, skilled workers could more than double that in enemy employment. For those with families to support and rent to pay, or those who needed to use the black market to make sure their children had enough to eat, it must have been a very strong temptation. It is a great irony that the defences built to keep Jersey people subjugated were built in some small part by members of that same community.

> Imagine you are a father with a wife and children to support, living in a flat in town with nowhere to grow your own food. They are starving and your small wage is simply not enough. Would you turn down the chance to double your pay so that you could supplement their diet with meat and milk from the Black Market?

But is it fair to accept the view of those historians who claim that Jersey's people and her government meekly accepted the Occupation and did little to oppose it? When Madeleine Bunting put forward that argument in her book *A Model Occupation*, there was outrage among those in the island who still remembered those dark days. They pointed to the twenty one islanders who are still commemorated every Holocaust Memorial Day, because they died or were killed in German camps for defying the Nazi regime.

People such as Canon Cohu, a clergyman beaten to death at Zöschen for spreading the BBC news, or father and son Clarence and Peter Painter who died after horrendous treatment at Gross-Rozen and Dora-Mittelbau. They had stolen German equipment and used an illicit radio.

And of course there were those whose brave acts of resistance went unheralded. Those who risked their lives sheltering escaped slaves, those who took flimsy little boats to get away and join the Allied forces, those who circulated seditious leaflets among German soldiers and incited them to rebel. While there certainly was collaboration by some in the island, many would argue that it was more than compensated for by the bravery and sacrifice of many others.

In the months after the Occupation ended there was much debate in the letters column of the *Evening Post* denouncing those who had taken the German *mark*. How should they be punished, they asked, how should they be brought to book?

The responses to a letter from a Mr M. Frowd perhaps illustrate the situation perfectly. He, describing himself as a 'Conchie', or conscientious objector, wrote to beg clemency for the women described as Jerrybags. "They have done no harm to anyone but themselves and their reputations," he wrote.

One anonymous response described too much conscience as '*a disease*', and contrasted those who had refused to take up arms to the brave Jersey men who had risked their lives in the forces in order to free the island. 'How grateful Mr Frowd must feel when he reads the words '*he gave his life for his friends*', the writer declared.

What he didn't know is that Mike Frowd had for months sheltered the escaped slave known as 'Russian Bill' in the attic of his flat, at huge risk to himself and his flatmate René Franoux who used to give language lessons to German soldiers in the living room. They knew only too well what would happen to them if they were caught, after Bill's previous hosts had been sent to concentration camps. Like many others, they had not considered it right or proper to trumpet their bravery when it was all over.

As the island recovered from the effects of the Occupation, there was a time of reckoning as those who believed they had behaved honourably sat in judgement on those who they believed had not. The issue still excites much comment, even now.

Perhaps in our free, well fed and relatively safe world with the benefit of time's perspective we should not be too hasty to judge those who chose to make their lives that little bit easier in a time of immense suffering. The future Prime Minister Anthony Eden was surely all too aware that if the Germans had managed to defeat Britain, then she *and* her people would have been faced with the same moral choices as those in the Channel Islands....

> "It would be impertinent for any country that has not suffered occupation
> to pass judgement on one that did."
> Anthony Eden

8 LOVE STORIES

"A young woman in love does not always weigh the consequences of her acts…."
Bailiff, Alexander Coutanche

While some 'Jerrybags' such as Ginger Lou may have flaunted their lovers for their influence and privileges, there were some genuine examples of island girls falling in love with German soldiers. While most ended sadly after Liberation, there were some whose tales reached a more dramatic end.

LOVE IS BLIND

Alice Thaureaux was just fifteen when the Occupation began, and she, like every other islander, endured five long years of privations and hardship at the hands of the Germans. But, as the saying goes, love is blind – and shortly before her twentieth birthday Alice fell passionately in love with a soldier.

Twenty three year old Nickolaus Schmitz may have been wearing the uniform of the enemy, but he was dark haired and handsome, and seemed to love Alice as much as she loved him. In the last few months of the war, as the Nazi empire collapsed, they clung to each other as the island waited for liberation.

But Nickolaus became disillusioned with the army, and wanted to spend all his time with his new love. Despairing of the grim outlook for himself and his comrades, he deserted and went into hiding with Alice.

Sadly, just a short time before Liberation, they were caught and thrown into prison. A military court martial condemned them both to death; him for deserting, and Alice for harbouring him.

On the 25 April 1945 the bailiff Alexander Coutanche wrote an emotional letter to the *Platzcomandant*, pleading mercy for her. She had been, he said, 'passionately in love' with Nickolaus, and had not harboured him for any political reason.

Perhaps realising the imminent collapse of Germany, the court accepted the appeal, and her sentence was reduced to a term in prison – which would of course come to an end very soon.

Nickolaus though was doomed. On the 27 April 1945, just three days before

A doomed love - Nickolaus
Schmitz and Alice Thaureaux

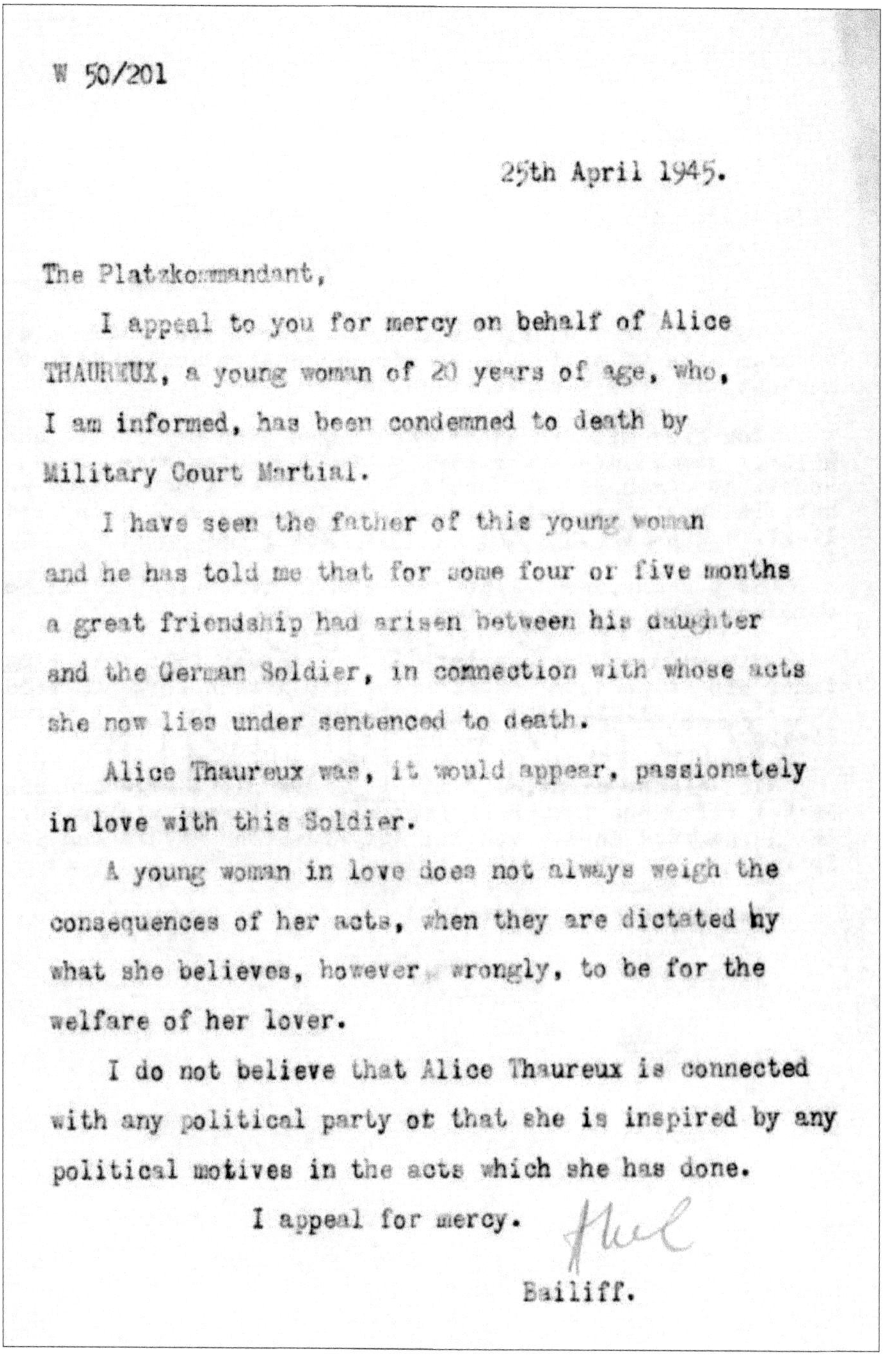

W 50/201

25th April 1945.

The Platzkommandant,

I appeal to you for mercy on behalf of Alice THAUREUX, a young woman of 20 years of age, who, I am informed, has been condemned to death by Military Court Martial.

I have seen the father of this young woman and he has told me that for some four or five months a great friendship had arisen between his daughter and the German Soldier, in connection with whose acts she now lies under sentenced to death.

Alice Thaureux was, it would appear, passionately in love with this Soldier.

A young woman in love does not always weigh the consequences of her acts, when they are dictated by what she believes, however wrongly, to be for the welfare of her lover.

I do not believe that Alice Thaureux is connected with any political party ot that she is inspired by any political motives in the acts which she has done.

I appeal for mercy.

Bailiff.

Courtesy of Jersey Heritage

The letter that saved Alice's life

Hitler committed suicide in Berlin, the young man was led to his death through the gates of Jersey prison. Alice could see him from her barred window, and waved her handkerchief to him in a last gesture of hopeless love. He was shot on the parade ground of Fort Regent.

A HAPPY ENDING: LOVERS ON SARK

There was a far happier ending to the story of a soldier and his lover on the smaller island of Sark. Werner Rang was a medical orderly who came to the Channel Islands in October 1941. He spent the next four years treating military personnel and civilians in Guernsey and Sark and described Sark as a 'little island paradise'.

One of his patients was young Phyllis Baker, who was suffering with tonsillitis. She remembers letting him in to the house using the German she had learnt at school. He later told her it was love at first sight, even though she was wrapped in towels and very unwell! Werner soon became a regular visitor to the farm where she lived.

But the war ended before things could progress any further. While many of his countrymen were held in the islands to get rid of all the mines, barbed wire and other defences, Werner was taken to England to be held as a prisoner of war. Allowed to send only one postcard, he chose to address it to Phyllis. When the rules relaxed, he wrote to her as often as possible, a hundred and sixty letters altogether, and she replied with a hundred of her own. Just before he was due to be sent home to East Germany, Phyllis managed to visit him in the camp – and they became engaged and very quickly married. It meant he could stay in the country.

After some unpleasant comments from people unhappy that she should choose to marry someone who until recently was an enemy, the couple moved back to Sark where they enjoyed a long and happy marriage. Werner ran the island's small ambulance service, built a home, and established a successful business which helped them to become part of the island community.

Werner would often tell people 'the only appreciation I can express to Hitler is to thank him for sending me here.'

> Is it possible for love to be blind in such circumstances? Could you have defied your family, friends and fellow islanders to be with your lover, even if he was the enemy?

9 ACTION

While Britain wisely decided against any attempt to re-take the Channel Islands, there was nonetheless plenty of military action in the seas and skies around Jersey – and even on the island itself.

The Royal Navy was a constant threat to the Germans' peace of mind, and the RAF was always making a nuisance of itself. Ships of both sides were sunk in island waters, aircraft shot down in island skies – and commandos even made an abortive raid on its shores.

PT509 – WAR AT SEA

One of the most dramatic battles came on the night of the 8 August 1944, at the south west tip of the island. A convoy of German ships had left St Peter Port in Guernsey in thick fog, carrying men and guns destined for Jersey. Two large freighters and eight heavily armed escort vessels made their way south through the darkness under the command of *Kapitänleutnant* Armin Zimmerman. Unknown to them, a flotilla of five American torpedo boats was stalking them eight miles to the west of Corbière. As well as torpedos, they carried depth charges and heavy machine guns and posed a real threat to any enemy ship they could find.

The fog became so thick that the German vessels put their searchlights on, scared of colliding with each other or the treacherous rocks around the Jersey coast. They were picked up on the radar of the prowling PT boats, which started to fire their torpedos. They fired at long range though, of up to three thousand yards – and missed. The commander of PT 509 then closed the distance, using his radar to come racing up alongside the armed trawler M4626, and started to blaze away at the vessel with his heavy machine guns. The Germans, of course, fired back.

In the chaos of the fire fight, the wheelman of PT 509 was badly hit, and the torpedo boat crashed hard into the side of the German gunship. Its engines still racing, the smaller boat's hull was smashed as it became wedged against the trawler's deck. Men on both sides kept up furious fire, as the Germans tried to push the torpedo boat away, afraid that its explosives and unfired torpedo could go up at any moment. Finally, as its engines coughed to a standstill, German sailors managed to jump on board and throw the dangerous munitions over the side before pushing it away from their own boat with iron bars. PT 509 drifted away into the fog before a huge explosion echoed across the sea. The damaged boat, carrying its injured crew, had blown up and sunk in moments.

The other PT boats came into the battle, firing more torpedos and their heavy guns at the German convoy, before finally breaking off the engagement. The convoy could only make it into St Helier harbour after two of its ships had been pulled free from rocks where they'd become grounded during the battle.

Fourteen men were killed from PT 509, and two from PT 503. 509's only survivor, John Page, was treated for his wounds and then held prisoner at a small camp on South Hill in St Helier.
Four Germans were killed and forty one wounded.
Three German ships were taken out of action.

The engagement happened so close to the coast that people living in the island heard and even saw some of the fighting. Edward Le Quesne was one witness....

"Early this morning I jumped out of bed having heard peculiar noises coming from the sea. Looking out of my window I saw a bank of dense fog and little else. Suddenly the fog lifted and there lay three ships almost on the rocks at Ouaisne Bay. They were backing off when suddenly one blew up. In a flash she was no more, neither did I see any survivors."

Diary of Edward Le Quesne, 8 August 1944

PT 509 remains on the sea bed just off Corbière. Her remains were found by a local diver in 1981.

In the year 2000 Shelton Bosley, a surviving crew member of PT 507 which had also seen action that night, returned to Jersey and dived down to the wreckage to remember his lost comrades. He also visited the memorial to the battle which is on the headland at Noirmont Point. Ironically, one of the large guns mounted in the restored bunkers at Noirmont was brought to the island by the convoy which the torpedo boats attacked.

JERSEY AND THE GREAT ESCAPE

On 18 November 1942, Free French RAF pilot Bernard Scheidhauer was on patrol in his Spitfire over Normandy. The sortie was what they called a 'rhubarb' – a chance to look for any German target of opportunity, and attack it.

Unfortunately for him though, he was hit by flak near Carentan which damaged his fuel lines and made the aircraft lose height fast. Streaking across the Cherbourg peninsula, he saw the sea – and a small island.

The battle had smashed his compass and played tricks on his sense of direction. He believed he was heading north and the island before him was the Isle of Wight, but he was actually heading west, and the island was Jersey. He finally wrestled his damaged aircraft down to land in a potato field in the north east of the island, very close to where the zoo is today.

> "The machine was only slightly damaged in landing, and although the pilot
> had to wait for a long time (over half an hour) for some Germans to appear
> to whom he could give himself up, he did not destroy it. It is said a farmer
> was asked for the necessary inflammables and either could not, or would not,
> oblige…. It is a pity the machine was allowed to get into Jerry hands intact."
>
> *Diary of Philip Le Sauteur*, 18 November 1942

Before long Scheidhauer was taken across the sea to France, ending up in the notorious Stalag Luft III prison camp in Silesia. It was a camp for Allied airmen who were known to be troublemakers, serial escapers or a risk to the Nazi regime. The Germans, rather foolishly, described it as escape proof.

Here he was surrounded by people whose only thought was to get away, and soon he joined the most audacious escape of all time. Seventy six officers got out of the camp through a tunnel in what became known as The Great Escape. He was paired with the leader of the breakout, Squadron Leader Roger Bushell.

But his luck wasn't to last. He was recaptured in Saarbrücken, supposedly after responding in English to a German soldier who accosted him. The incident was recreated in the famous film, where a German wishes Gordon Jackson's character 'Good luck'.

There was no happy ending for Pilot Officer Scheidhauer. He was one of the fifty escapers who were killed on the orders of Adolf Hitler, who was outraged that such a large scale escape could happen. Together with Roger Bushell, he was driven into remote woodland and shot; the Germans claimed he had been 'trying to escape'.

There had been no escape for his Spitfire, either. The Germans dragged it out of the field in Trinity where it had landed, and managed to restore it to flying condition. They took it to their testing site at Echterdingen and removed the Merlin engine from the nose, replacing it with the Daimler Benz engine which was used to power their own FW 109s. They painted it in Luftwaffe camouflage and took it on high performance tests. They found that the hybrid aircraft (since rechristened the 'Messerspit') handled better than their own fighters on the ground and at low level, and also achieved a higher ceiling. German pilots were known to queue to get their hands on the iconic aircraft.

It was finally destroyed in Allied bombing raids.

On 17 September 1999, a plaque remembering P/O Bernard Scheidhauer was unveiled close to the place where he crashed. Survivors of the Great Escape came to Jersey for the occasion, among them Sydney Dowse who had been the third man out of the tunnel and a friend of Roger Bushell. As a bugler played the Last Post, a lone Spitfire roared overhead in an emotional flypast.

Jersey's airport was used as a forward base for aircraft taking part in the Blitz on England. While the runway may have been too short for the biggest bombers, fighter escorts would refuel there before joining the attack. But it wasn't always easy for them. At the height of the Battle of Britain, Philip Le Sauteur noted the effect the fighting was having....

".... of the 14 pilots who planned a celebration lunch on Thursday for when they returned from their blitz, only one appeared at the appointed time and place.... and he sat through the time with his head in his hands."

Diary of Philip Le Sauteur, 18 August 1940

A TYPHOON OVER JERSEY

On 14 June 1944, very soon after D-Day, Squadron Leader Henri Gonay took off from England leading a formation of eight Hawker Typhoons. His mission was to attack any suitable German target which could menace the invasion. They found two enemy vessels sailing off the coast of Jersey and attacked, but accurate anti-aircraft fire came pouring back at them and S/Ldr Gonay's aircraft was fatally damaged. It stuttered on over Jersey, losing height rapidly, heading straight for a farm house in St Ouen. Three year old Brian Follain was being given a wash in the kitchen sink and his brother was playing outside when his mother heard the aircraft approaching....

"My mother grabbed me from the sink and ran outside.... just in time to see a crippled plane heading straight towards the back yard where Graeme was playing. My mother picked up Graeme and ran with both of us to the front door of the farmhouse. The aircraft crashed and burst into flames, killing the pilot. The house immediately caught fire and we scrambled out. My family lost all possessions. We were penniless and only had the clothes we stood up in."

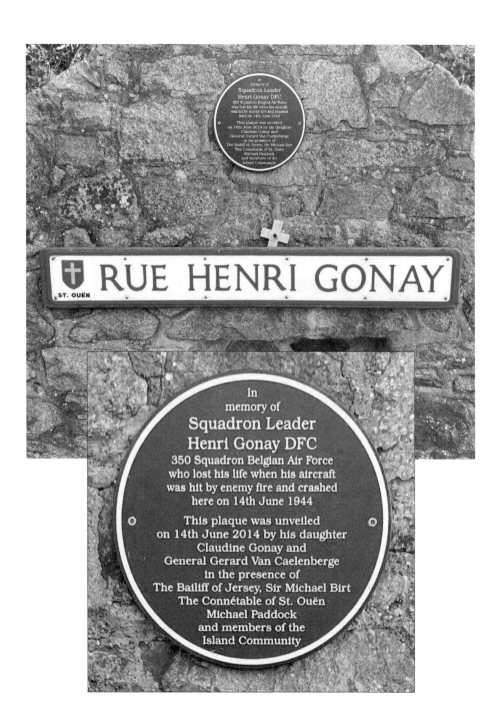

Many aircraft were shot down over Jersey, such as this
American Thunderbolt which came down after D-Day

Brian's family and other local people remembered the pilot's bravery by re-naming the road La Rue Henri Gonay, and there is a commemorative plaque on the site where it happened.

THE RAID – COMMANDOS ON JERSEY

One of the reasons Hitler issued his command to turn the Channel Islands into fortresses was that he was convinced the British would try to take them back. Why would they not want to reclaim them, he reasoned, as the sole part of their territory occupied by the enemy? But the British gave very little consideration to that idea. They, perhaps fortunately, realised that the islands would be very difficult to re-take – and after that almost impossible to hold, given their location so close to German-occupied France. Despite some thinly constructed plans, which were dreamt up by the creator of James Bond, Ian Fleming, Churchill and his military leaders were more than happy for the Germans to waste tons of resources and thousands of men defending islands which were of no real strategic use to the Allied war effort.

But that didn't mean that they weren't curious; and they wanted to know just what resources the Germans had diverted to the islands and how they had fortified them. What they found out could give vital clues to how the defences were organised in other places such as the coast of Normandy. So it was that a series of raids were planned to investigate each island. Sadly, none of them were particularly successful.

On Christmas Day 1943, a group of commandos under the command of twenty two year old Captain Philip Ayton landed on a small beach on the north coast of Jersey known as Petit Port. It was (and is) a rugged place of overbearing cliffs and dense gorse, but it had the advantage of being almost unobserved by any German emplacement. Captain Ayton and his men stopped first at the little stone hut called Wolf's Lair before climbing up the rocky track towards the road above the cliffs. The first buildings they found were part of the old settlement of Egypt, which the Germans had partly demolished to use as a site for training in house to house fighting. Avoiding minefields, they then searched some abandoned German positions before knocking on the door of the first occupied home they saw, called La Geonnière. But the people who lived there were convinced they were Germans causing trouble, and sent them on their way.

The Commandos had better luck at the next house they tried. The Le Breton brothers, John and Hedley, let them in once they had overcome their shock at being confronted by British soldiers in uniform. The brothers told them all they knew about the German garrison on the island and their defences.

Captain Ayton and his men scouted briefly for an occupied German position so they could learn more, and perhaps snatch a prisoner, but time was running out for their pickup by boat at the beach. As they made their way back down the hill, tragedy struck. Captain Ayton stood on a mine and was badly injured in the explosion. In the ensuing chaos the soldiers managed to rescue him and make their haphazard way back down to the beach and rescue, expecting to hear German gunfire at their backs at any moment. Luckily for them it never came, and they managed to escape. Sadly Captain Ayton died later that day.

There is a permanent memorial to the Captain and his men next to Wolf's Lair, and a small service every year remembers their actions.

SARK, DAVID NIVEN, AND THE COMMANDO ORDER

As well as the raid on Jersey, British Commandos also landed on some of the other Channel Islands. The raid on Guernsey was in July 1940, shortly after the Occupation began. After a brave solo reconnaissance by Guernsey man Lieutenant Hubert Nicolle, plans were made for one hundred and forty Commandos to land on the island under the command of Lieutenant Colonel Hugh Durnford-Slater. He worked on details of the plan with the famous actor David Niven, who had withdrawn from the glamour of Hollywood to serve his country as an officer in Combined Operations.

The raid, one of the earliest of the war, was a fiasco. The plan was for one group to cause a diversion while the main company attacked any German targets at the airfield. In the event, only the forty strong diversionary group was able to land on target. The others ended up in Sark, where they found nothing of interest and withdrew. Those who had managed to land in Guernsey found only some abandoned positions before cutting a telephone wire and heading back to the beach for their pickup. When they got there they found that the tide had risen, meaning their boats were a hundred yards out to sea – and three of the men couldn't swim. They were left behind to be captured as the rest of the men made a rather ignominious return to the destroyer waiting for them offshore. It is said that Churchill was less than impressed.

Two years later, the Commandos returned to the Channel Islands, this time aiming particularly at Sark, one of the smallest. The first attempt at Operation Basalt was abandoned on the night of 18 September 1942, because of delays caused by the sea conditions. But on the night of 3 October, twelve men landed successfully at a spot called The Hog's Back. Scaling the cliffs, they broke into a house whose owner was happy to give them as much information as possible. She sent them to the nearby Dixcart Hotel, which was a billet for German soldiers. One commando killed a guard, while the other raiders seized five other soldiers as prisoners. What they did next would have important consequences for any Allied soldier on future covert missions in enemy territory; they tied their prisoners hands, and took away their belts and braces so they had to hold their trousers up. It was a quick means of making sure they couldn't run away, leaving the commandos to look for more positions and intelligence. But while the attackers were occupied, one of the bound men tried to escape. That led to a struggle, and while he got away three of the others were shot as they tried to run for it when the commandos tried to force them back down to the beach. Only one prisoner, *Obergefreiter* Hermann Weinreich, made it down to the waiting boats and back across the sea to England.

Operation Basalt had been rather more successful than the raids on Jersey and Guernsey, and when he got to hear about it Adolf Hitler was furious. What angered him the most was that it came just days after the much larger attack on Dieppe, a brave if very costly attempt to see just how a seaborne force would fare against the Germans shore defences. In the Dieppe raid too, it was claimed, the attackers had been instructed to tie the hands of any prisoners they took. Hitler had already promised reprisals for what he saw as action against the correct treatment of prisoners laid out in the Geneva Convention; and when details of the Sark raid emerged he issued his infamous '*Kommandobefehl*', or Commando Order. From now on, he decreed, any Allied special forces soldier that was taken prisoner should be executed immediately, without the benefit of a trial. From that moment on, any man volunteering for Commando or similar units would do so knowing that he would never survive capture.

The raids on the islands also taught the Allies some important lessons about how to mount successful covert operations against occupied territory, which they later put to good use on D-Day.

ESCAPE AND ASSAULT: THE RAID ON GRANVILLE

The second week of March 1945 was a dramatic one for Jersey. On the 7th the Palace Hotel in St Saviour blew up, after a German deserter set fire to an ammunition store. The explosions and flames could be seen and heard in St Helier.

But the destruction of the hotel didn't divert the plans of the German officers who had been plotting in its rooms an ambitious attack of their own. Together, they came up with a daring and very successful raid – thanks to some brave escapers. Four German soldiers and a sailor were being held prisoner by the Americans in Granville, a small harbour town 50km to the south east of Jersey. After being set to work at the port helping to unload plentiful supplies of coal and ammunition, they resolved to escape and share their intelligence about the enemy with the Channel Islands authorities. Bravely they managed to get out of their camp and steal a boat from under the Americans' noses, which they sailed to Jersey before telling everything they knew to *Vizeadmiral* Hüffmeier. He was an ardent Nazi who longed to take the fight to the Allies but he also knew the value of coal and other resources to his beleaguered garrison. At the Palace Hotel, he and his officers drew up a plan.

On the night of the 8-9 March 1945, a flotilla of gun boats set out from St Helier harbour and headed south east towards Granville. They managed to fool the outer defences and land without a shot being fired, before storming ashore and attacking the port buildings and other ships. The landing party ran amok killing soldiers, mining ships and sabotaging the lock mechanism before trying to get away with ships full of coal. The problem was that the tide had gone out a long way and they only managed to get away with one coal-bearing vessel. They brought back with them some Germans who had been held in the nearby prisoner of war camp, and some American prisoners of their own who were dazed by the unexpected and ferocious attack.

Dr Noel Youngren was one of the Americans who was taken. He remembered going to bed in Granville after a rich supper before being rudely awakened by the fighting and before he knew it, he was being pushed onto a German boat and taken to Jersey.

"We didn't know what in Hades was going on. We didn't think there was a
German within 200 miles of us. It was a complete shock."

Philip Le Sauteur heard about it from the BBC news, which said there was a Commando raid on Granville, 'probably' from the Channel Islands. He had been wondering why there had been so much 'rumbling and banging' out to sea in the early hours. He observed the arrival of the newly liberated German POWs, who weren't looking too cheerful because they knew they'd end up being taken prisoner again and meanwhile had been brought to a place where there wasn't much grub. He also noted how the men who had carried out the raid were rewarded....

"The men taking part were presented with an Iron Cross of whatever class their
rank earned them, a packet of 20 cigarettes and pot of sugar beet syrup. One
wonders which reward was most valued."

Diary of Philip Le Sauteur, 14 March 1945

118

The Americans who had been taken prisoner in the raid were taken to the POW camp at South Hill, adjacent to the gym and located where Jersey's learner drivers now practise their skills. Barbed wire and brushwood fences kept them isolated and deprived them of a view of the sea. It didn't stop the locals from contacting them though, either by hiding little packages of food in the wall or in one case passing messages hidden in the handlebars of their bikes.

There were already some of their countrymen there who had been captured in various other battles in France, and they had already celebrated a 'Great Escape' of their own. Early in January 1945 two officers, Captain Ed Clark and First Lieutenant George Haas, first tried to dig a tunnel under the latrine but were caught. Haas was sent to prison in St Helier where he managed to communicate with some of the islanders who were being held there for various offences against the occupiers, and they gave him suggestions of who might be able to help in his next attempt.

He didn't wait long. Together with Captain Clark, he fashioned a ladder and managed to scale the wall at the back of the camp to the east before slipping along the coast road to their first safe house. The Laurens family helped them with food and clothing until they decided to move on to the next name they had on their list, that of Bill Bertram at a house called East Lynne on the East coast. He and his family, like the Laurens, were very happy to help despite the German proclamation that anyone who assisted the escapers would be put to death.

After several days they crept into Gorey harbour before stealing a boat and rowing across rough seas to France where they were reunited with their comrades two weeks after getting out of their prison compound.

While Jersey may not have been invaded, and so avoided the terrible consequences of a land battle, it was nonetheless a place which often saw frantic action of other kinds. All across the island, if you look closely enough, you can still see the evidence of bombing, strafing and captivity; while the seas around the south west coast in particular hold the wrecks of many German boats which fell victim to Allied attack or accident. Men – and women – died in many actions which give the lie to the notion that it was a 'peaceful' Occupation.

Funeral of RAF Sergeants Dennis Butlin and Abraham Holden, shot down in 1943.
The Germans granted them full military honours to show respect
to the local population

121

10 AGENT ZIGZAG: THE JERSEY CONNECTION

Eddie Chapman was a notorious safe breaker, jewel thief – and one of the most extraordinary double-agents of the second world war. Wanted in London for theft before hostilities began, he and his girlfriend fled to Jersey on 7 February 1939 to escape arrest. They stayed at the Hotel de la Plage at Havre des Pas, but the police weren't far behind. Officers tried to arrest Chapman in the middle of dinner but he jumped out of the hotel dining room, ran along the promenade, and escaped. After burgling a local nightclub, he was finally caught and thrown into the island prison. He managed to escape, and stole explosives from a quarry at L'Etacq so that he could return to his life of crime.

Disguised as a fisherman, he was eventually arrested on the beach at Plémont. He had visited the clifftop tea rooms there, whose owner recognised him from the newspaper. She alerted the police. They found him on the sand watching a game of football, while brandishing a large shrimping net. There was a chase, a fight, and they ran him to ground inside one of the large caves where he struggled until he was recaptured.

Back in prison, he was working on another escape when the war began, and not long after that the Germans invaded. Eddie Chapman was still behind bars when the bombs fell on St Helier, and the first soldiers marched down The Parade.

Finally released on 15 October 1941, he 'worked' in a hairdressers shop in St Helier which was used as a front for black marketeering, but it didn't satisfy his craving for excitement – and freedom. Together with an accomplice he wrote to the German authorities with an extraordinary offer: he would become a secret agent for them.

For weeks nothing happened, until he was wrongly accused of cutting some telephone wires and sent to prison in France. Under interrogation he insisted he wanted to strike back at the British system which had so often imprisoned him; and finally he overcame their suspicions.

He was trained in essential spycraft, codes and communications and parachuted into England on a mission to destroy an aircraft factory; but he immediately contacted the police, an unexpected step for a man still wanted for many serious crimes. He offered instead to spy for the British.

That led to an extraordinary game of double cross, as Chapman helped to fake the destruction of the aircraft factory and with British help managed to return to Germany where he was actually given a job teaching the art of spying. He was even given the Iron Cross for his work!

Eddie Chapman was the only British citizen to be awarded the Iron Cross.

After the invasion of Normandy the Germans called on his skills again. They sent him to report on the accuracy of the flying bombs which were blasting off from northern France to bombard London. Once again Chapman went straight to the British authorities, and they devised a way to trick the Germans into aiming their bombs slightly short of the centre of the capital. He may have saved hundreds of lives.

He never returned to Germany, but stayed on in England immersed once more in the London underworld. MI5 paid him off, and pardoned him for his pre-war crimes.

He was the subject of the film *Triple Cross* starring Christopher Plummer, as well as several books and TV programmes.

Eddie Chapman
captured by the
Jersey Police
in 1939

11   HUNGER AND WANT

"It hurts when you're really hungry. My mother had given me a small piece of swede – raw swede. I remember eating it and, at the same time, feeling guilty because I knew it was the next day's food."

Jennie Seymour

Perhaps the prevailing memory of anyone who lived through the Occupation of the Channel Islands is hunger. In seems unimaginable in this modern age of plenty that the people of a previously prosperous British island could be reduced to scavenging for any little scrap, eating bread made with sawdust and paying extortionate amounts for something as simple as an egg on the black market. But before they were finally liberated, Channel Islanders were reduced almost to starvation.

The main reason for this was simple geography. Jersey is an island nine miles by five, at least fifteen miles from the nearest land and further still from any significant harbour. As the Germans took essentials from the island to help feed their vast armies in Europe, it just couldn't be replaced fast enough to feed more than forty thousand people and ten thousand troops. And when the Allies took Cherbourg and St Malo, it was left to fend for itself in one of the coldest winters in recent history. "Let 'em starve." wrote Churchill on a memo about the situation in the islands. Its never been made clear whether he meant everyone, or just the Germans, but the effect was the same.

Both the Jersey authorities and the Germans recognised that some kind of rationing would be necessary right from the start. It began just days after the first Germans arrived.

Butter, tea and coffee, salt, cocoa and cooking fats were all limited.

You could get twelve ounces of meat per week. To put that into context, that would be enough for three regular hamburgers today.

All of these things would become increasingly rare commodities as the Occupation wore on, and the weekly allocation of all of them was steadily cut. Jersey reached an agreement to buy supplies from France, but it would never be enough.

Potatoes, for so long a staple of the Jersey diet, were rationed from 1942 after the crops failed. Milk production was carefully monitored by the Germans to make sure they got their quota before the farmers could sell it on.

What tinned food and few luxuries people were able to find were either hoarded away, or eaten if they were perishable; and from then on things became increasingly hard. There was little point in going shopping unless it was to collect your rations, as shelves were quickly emptied of anything that might be edible. Occasionally word would go around that a certain shop had managed to acquire a small shipment of cheese or tins of fruit, and queues would form instantly until the rare commodity was snapped up.

Farmers hid livestock to prevent it from being taken to feed the enemy.

As the reality of their situation became increasingly apparent, islanders became more and more inventive in finding things to eat and drink. With imagination, hard work and a strong stomach, it was possible to create *ersatz* alternatives for the things they missed.

Ersatz: German; a replacement or substitute for the regular item. Eg coffee, tea, flour. Commonly used when regular items are unavailable.

Real tea for example reached astronomical prices on the black market, up to twenty five pounds for a bag when the weekly wage was three pounds. The ration for tea had been cut to zero in December 1941. Those desperate for their morning brew would spend days picking blackberry leaves, parsley or nettles to be painstakingly dried and then crushed to make an *ersatz* version of their favourite drink.

Coffee was also almost impossible to come by, but an acceptable alternative could be made by roasting acorns and then grinding them in the same way as coffee beans.

Sugar meant boiling down sugar beet for hours until it formed a sludgy paste which would then be squeezed through cloth to strain out the pulp. It was then boiled again to make a syrup which could be added to puddings or drinks.

Flour was a necessity if people were to have bread, but without sufficient imports of wheat it became almost impossible to find. Instead, islanders found that they could make something similar by peeling, crushing and then drying potatoes, an arduous and time consuming process. In her diary, Nan Le Ruez frequently wrote about her flour-making duties....

August 13, 1941
"Rainy and cold all day. Alice and Amy and I scrubbed 550 pounds of potatoes in the shed in the little yard. Francis took them to Mr de Gruchy at St Mary where in ten minutes they were all crushed to a pulp! We put all the pulp in a big tub and covered it for the night."

Dinner!

Soldiers tried to supplement their diets with fish

Counting the crops before taking their share

A lucky catch

August 14, 1941

"Pouring rain all day. Herbert and I squeezed potato pulp in the pantry all morning."

August 16, 1941

"Sun was shining this morning so I put out all the flour to dry.... Spent most of day re-washing pulp of yesterday (the third time). Weighed last week's flour. We had 9 pounds out of 120 pounds of potatoes – not enough!"

Diary of Nan Le Ruez

Even the most fussy eaters became used to bland, repetitive food that had no other appeal other than keeping them alive from one hungry day to the next. Daphne Minihane remembers that dinner was usually referred to as S.O.S. – 'Same Old Swede'!

Recipes became more and more unusual, and some who were children still remember certain things they had to eat....

Grey bread with sugar beet syrup

Potato Pap

Lentil soup

Boiled pigeon

Starling soup

Ersatz sausage

Limpet stew made with diluted sea water

A kind of blancmange made from seaweed

Swede. Always swede. If you were lucky, it was cooked.

Those who lived in town suffered far more than those who lived in the country or on the farm. Simply, if you lived in a flat in St Helier there was nowhere for you to plant your own little stock of potatoes or other vegetables, nowhere to keep a chicken for eggs or a cow for milk.

It wasn't always easy for farmers either though. They were subject to snap inspections by the Germans, who kept records of all the livestock and expected yields of milk, meat and crops. They couldn't simply kill a pig to eat or sell, because the Germans would expect to take it. There are many apocryphal tales of frantic attempts to hide various animals when soldiers paid an unexpected visit. The most common involves the farmer and his sons dragging the freshly slaughtered animal up the stairs to the mother's room and tucking it under the bedclothes, then explaining to the curious Germans that 'Mother isn't feeling very well....!'

Bob Le Sueur tells of a solemn and mournful funeral procession which wound its way from St Saviour to town, complete with a glass-sided, horse-drawn hearse. Some German soldiers even doffed their hats as it passed. After making its doleful way into the funeral parlour, the coffin was opened by the undertaker, to reveal a newly butchered pig ready to be shared out among people who could afford to pay for it.

Bob also remembers taking part in a theatrical production at the Opera House. One scene in the second act was set in a farmhouse, where the farmer's wife was to be seen peeling a swede. During rehearsals, she mimed. On the first night, two ACTUAL swedes were put carefully on the props table....

"Yet when the scene began, the actress appeared on stage bereft of vegetables of any description and resorted once again to her well practised dumb show. .... after the curtain came down, there were urgent questions about what had happened to our edible props. Finally, shamefacedly, two members of the cast admitted that in the time between the swedes being put on the props table and the show starting, they had eaten them. Raw."

Bob Le Sueur, *Growing Up Fast*

A need for food led to many townsfolk making foraging expeditions into the country to see what they might be able to find. A favourite pastime was 'gleaning'. That meant going to a farmer's field immediately after he had finished his harvest and seeing if there were any potatoes or ears of corn left in the soil. People might expend hundreds of precious calories to ride or walk to far off fields only to find that others had got there before them and there was nothing left. They would have to be very patient and hard working to glean enough produce to make the journey worthwhile, and often quick to avoid the farmers themselves who wanted to make sure their crops were safely gathered.

In Guernsey, where the pre-war crop had relied mainly on tomatoes, potatoes were in even shorter supply. Long queues would form at the market when merchants were allowed to sell the peelings from their occupiers' dinners. The popularity of potato peel pie became the inspiration for the recent novel *The Guernsey Literary and Potato Peel Pie Society* by Mary Ann Shaffer.

While anyone with a garden might be able to grow some vegetables to supplement their rations, the hardest job was to source protein. With milk rationed and cows, pigs and chickens all accounted for, it was difficult to keep muscles working and bones healthy. While Jersey's waters are known for the quality of their fish, the

Germans were understandably reluctant to allow boats to leave the island in case the crews tried to escape. Nevertheless they did recognise that fish could provide essential proteins and oils, so they allowed some out under strict conditions.

They had to stay within sight of the shore, and they had to have an escort of soldiers – as well as patrolling boats nearby. Skippers also had to pay a hefty deposit against the value of their boat, and give over a large part of their catch to the German garrison.

Shellfish were more easily accessible, as contrary to popular belief islanders were allowed access to most beaches for most of the war. (They became more strictly controlled after D-Day.)

As the tides went out, figures in thick coats and heavy boots would be seen trudging down to the rocks to pry off limpets and other creatures which could be boiled into a rather smelly and chewy stew. Others set nets at high water which would trap any fish unlucky enough to be caught as the tide went out.

In late 1944, once the Allies had landed in Normandy and cut off the French ports, things became even worse. Nothing could come to the island from France, and both islanders and occupiers had to live on what was left. Rations were cut further and the daily calorie intake dropped steadily, until for some it came down to around a thousand a day. The requirement for a healthy man is around two thousand five hundred.

The meat ration dropped from twelve ounces a week at the start of the Occupation to just two by January 1945. That's half a modern hamburger. The four ounce sugar ration had completely run out.

Even the Black Market dried up as people scrabbled to find anything they could put in their mouths.

"Xmas, perhaps the most distressing of the Occupation. Nothing in the shops for the kiddies. Bad news from the front. Prices soared on what there was on the Black Market....

Rabbits £2 to £4 each.
Geese £9 to £12 each.
Turkeys £14 to £20 each."

Diary of Edward Le Quesne, 23 December 1944

With the weekly wage in Jersey set at £3, it meant paying a week's income for a single rabbit – in modern terms, around £600!

Soon even if they could find some swedes, carrots or other kind of sustenance, they couldn't even cook it. In December there was no more gas. In January the electricity was cut off. Whole families would sit with pinched and gaunt faces to a dinner of raw vegetables with whatever else they had managed to scavenge. This led to unexpected consequences....

"....the complete lack of restraint, even in company, of breaking wind. It is really funny how people, who five years ago would not have dreamt of making rude noises in public, now do so without blush or apology...."

Diary of Philip Le Sauteur, 3 January 1945

For a while there were communal bakehouses, where ovens were kept going with fire wood, until the supplies of that ran out too. They were desperate times.

The Germans themselves were in equally dire straits. Their supplies were just as short, and many soldiers went scavenging for extra food with sometimes deadly consequences. Simply, they stole what they wanted, despite the risk of being punished by their own officers.

"People faint for lack of proper food, many die suddenly of heart failure and one woman was shot last week by German soldiers when she went downstairs one night, and has died."

Diary of Nan Le Ruez, 2nd January 1945

The woman in question, a Miss Waddell, had disturbed some German soldiers who were trying to break into her home at Portelet. They had been in search of something to eat.

Sometimes they were even more blatant, arriving unexpectedly at remote farms and simply demanding milk, meat or bread. David Rabet's family's precious chickens were taken by one raiding party but they had to grin and bear it:

"In those days you didn't argue with a German who had a gun."

The slave workers were in an even more parlous state, and would sometimes escape from their camps overnight to raid homes and farms. A shopkeeper in St Mary was killed when he went downstairs in the middle of the night to find a gang of Russians ransacking his property.

By December 1944 virtually everything that could be issued by the authorities had run out. You could get seven ounces of flour and two ounces of butter a week, although that was about to stop. There was no sugar and no salt. Theoretically you could get four pounds and four ounces of bread, but that was so padded out with sawdust and chaff that it had very little nutritional benefit. You had to rely on what you could grow, swap, scavenge, steal – or buy on the black market.

Pet cats and dogs began to 'disappear'.

Behind the scenes, the Bailiff and the island authorities had not been idle. They had managed to report the situation to both the British government and the Red

Saved! the arrival of the SS *Vega*

Red Cross parcels and some of their contents

Cross. When that organisation requested permission to sail to the Channel Islands with aid, Churchill was dismissive at first amid fears it would be pilfered by the Germans.

But the occupiers gave their word that any Red Cross parcels sent to the islands would not be touched, and Churchill relented. As winter's icy hand reached out across the perishing island, the Red Cross cargo vessel SS *Vega* sailed from the neutral port of Lisbon crammed with provisions which would literally save the lives of many Channel Islanders. The Bailiffs of Jersey and Guernsey were able to tell their people that she was coming, and anticipation built to fever pitch.

RELIEF – THE ARRIVAL OF THE SS *VEGA*

On 27 December 1944, salvation came to the Channel Islands. The *Vega*, painted white and with prominent red crosses, steamed slowly into Guernsey's St Peter Port harbour, to a rapturous welcome from local people. From inside her holds came thousands of Red Cross parcels, made up by countries which were still enjoying relative plenty such as Canada and New Zealand.

On 30 December she arrived in Jersey, where her reception was equally joyous.

Whole families went to the harbour or to local shops to present their ration cards and be issued with their precious parcels. St John Ambulance took responsibility for their fair distribution.

For islanders the simple boxes, the size of a shoe box and covered in brown paper knotted with string, represented more than just food. It was a sign that the world had not forgotten them. After years of strict rationing, children in particular were able to enjoy treats they had scarcely dared to dream of.

The contents of each parcel varied according to which country had packed them.

Those from Canada contained:

5oz Chocolate, 12oz Biscuits, 3oz Sardines, 16oz Milk powder, 6oz Prunes, 8oz Salmon, 12oz Corned beef, 7oz Raisins, 8oz Sugar, 4oz Tea, 4oz Cheese, 16oz Marmalade, 16oz Butter, 10oz Spam, 3oz Soap and 1oz Pepper and salt

And if your parcel came from New Zealand you would find:

4oz Tea, 16oz Corned mutton, 12oz Lamb and green peas, 6oz Chocolate, 16oz Butter, 16oz Coffee and milk, 6oz Sugar, 7oz Peas, 14oz Jam, 16oz Honey, 12oz Cheese and 6oz Raisins

When you compare these modest amounts of food with the shopping trollies full of provisions we can get from a modern supermarket, they may seem tiny. But to the starving people of the Channel Islands, they were manna from heaven....

"How wonderful all the things are! It brings tears to one's eyes. One feels so grateful to all who've had a share in the making-up and delivering of all these good things for us. What have we done to deserve it!"

Diary of Nan Le Ruez 4 January 1945

People consumed the contents of their parcels according to their whim. While some cannily hoarded as much as possible, not knowing when the next supply might come, others could not restrain themselves from satisfying their cravings....

"I opened the lid to see a cardboard box crammed with all kinds of packets and tins, but the one which immediately grabbed my attention was marked 'Klim'. I knew that to be dried, sweetened, powdered milk. In a flash I had grabbed a spoon from the kitchen and began what can only be described as my Klim Orgy. Delving deeply I scooped out a huge heaped spoonful of powder and without hesitation crammed it straight into my mouth. My teeth were gummed together almost immediately, my tongue stuck to my palate and my whole mouth was one disgusting sticky, gooey mess. I could scarcely breathe. It was divine."

Bob Le Sueur, *Growing Up Fast*

Vega didn't just bring food parcels. On board too were cigarettes, dietary supplements, medical supplies and soap, all of which had virtually run out.

The arrival of the *Vega* was the turning point for the people of the Channel Islands.

Before she came, in the depths of winter, the dark nights were at their longest and the days were short and brutally cold. *Vega* didn't just bring supplies – she brought hope the war might soon be over, and as the days grew longer she returned several times with more. Her last visit, after Liberation, brought more parcels but also essentials such as boots, shoes and paraffin.

Altogether, the *Vega* brought almost half a million food parcels to the islands.

The people were so grateful that they immediately began a fund raising campaign to thank the Red Cross which in Jersey raised £125,000 by the end of October 1945.

To this day, the *Vega* is remembered with emotion by many islanders, and there is a memorial to her work on the Albert Pier where she docked.

Of course it wasn't just food that was in short supply during the Occupation years. Anything that would usually have to be brought in by sea was limited, as the Germans prioritised war *matériel* and provisions for their own garrison above luxuries such as clothing, footwear or cleaning products. It wasn't long before islanders found themselves short of many of life's essentials.

Children in particular suffered from a lack of properly fitting shoes as their feet grew. Many relied on pairs passed down from older siblings, or patching old pairs with cardboard. A factory opened at Summerland in Rouge Bouillon where two hundred and fifty people worked to make so called 'Summerland Clogs' from wooden soles with uppers cut from pieces of scavenged leather. Their *click-clack* sound became recognisable on pavements across the island – but they caused blisters and were very painful….

"We had these dreadful calf leather boots and mother used to put us in a bucket of warm water with the boots on to soak and mould to our feet. Then we had to run around the garden until they dried. And they were so, so uncomfortable."

Mary Moody

Again though there are stories of Germans helping out. One soldier asked the mother of the house if she had any further use for an old leather handbag. When she said no he took it, only to return later with a pair of hand stitched shoes for her young daughter.

Many remember with joy the visits of the Vega not just for the food parcels she brought but also the countless pairs of black lace-up boots, which became *de rigueur* for anyone whose shoes had been worn through to the lining.

Clothing was also rationed, and it was very hard to come by anything that wasn't strictly functional. Where once you could simply go to a high street shop and buy a new pair of trousers in your size, you would now have to wait until your existing pair started to fray and fall apart before finding some material to patch them with. Bob Le Sueur remembers a threadbare old suit selling for seven pounds at auction – more than twice the weekly wage.

Out of necessity, women became increasingly adept at making alterations and repairs, and finding cloth to create new garments. Old clothes were pressed back into service, and many pairs of curtains were refashioned into skirts or jackets. The factory at Summerland took in old blankets and sheets and transformed them into coats or shirts but there was never enough, especially during the terrible winter of 1944-45.

Some people found that as they lost weight their old jumpers no longer fitted them and they were simply unravelled to their constituent strands of wool and re-knitted into two 'new' ones. Others turned cardigans into socks.

Those who began the war with wardrobes full of good quality clothing found they could stay reasonably warm and presentable. But those who were impoverished in 1940 found themselves in a pitiful state as the Occupation wore on….

"A man working for us at tree-felling called on me today. He was without shirt, vest or underpants. His coat and trousers were only rags and his soleless shoes were tied to his feet with string. Two other old ladies called. They had been living on 10/- a week for some time and appeared starved and emaciated. These are only two instances of what four years of war have and are doing to the poor of the Island."

Diary of Edward Le Quesne, 14 January 1944

During the winter of 1944-45, as temperatures froze and power was cut off, it wasn't uncommon for people to wear almost their entire wardrobe to bed an attempt to keep warm.

The shortage of soap and other cleaning products didn't help. Not only did it mean that people themselves became more and more dirty, they were unable to clean their clothes. That accelerated the wearing process and gave many garments an unpleasant sheen and aroma. Not to put too fine a point on it, bodies and clothing often stank of sweat and over-use. Many survivors have spoken of going to the cinema to try to get warm, only to be greeted by a foul fug of body odour from the unwashed masses inside.

With no soap and no hot water, it was impossible to clean anything successfully – be that clothes, dishes, hair, work surfaces or cutlery. Some remember washing in the sea when it began to warm up in spring 1945, only to need a rinse with fresh water to take the salt off.

While pans could be scoured with handfuls of twigs or a scoop of sand or gravel from the beach, many everyday objects acquired a patina of dirt that would only be scrubbed off after the *Vega* appeared with cakes of soap in every parcel.

The upper classes suffered just as much as the others. On Liberation Day, when the Bailiff Alexander Coutanche boarded the Royal Navy ship HMS *Beagle* to witness the signing of the surrender, he remarked how wonderful it was to be able to wash his hands with real soap again. The bemused captain ordered his crew to issue Coutanche, a representative of His Majesty the King, with a cake all of his own.

The shortage of fuel caused all kinds of problems. In that long winter, islanders had to survive for weeks without electricity or gas. That meant no hot water. No cooking. No heating. No light. Families would sit down to whatever poor meal they could put together before the sun went down not long after four o'clock, and then simply go to bed because there wasn't enough light to do anything else. Washing up often had to wait until the water was turned on again.

Some managed to hoard enough candles to give themselves a little light; but the candles themselves had to be lit with something, and some found themselves down to their last few matches which were held as prized possessions.

It was desperately cold too, in that last winter. The only source of fuel were the island's trees, many of which had been cut down at the start of the Occupation to create clear fields of fire for German guns. Later it was strictly forbidden to cut down any more, but both sides ignored the order simply to stay warm. Young Roland Carter said it was his 'life's work' to find scraps of wood for the family stove....

"One day the Germans felled all the trees on St Lawrence main road, and it was like manna from heaven. The Germans with their cross-cuts were sawing up the logs and taking them away and my sisters and I were busy heaping them into our cart without the Germans spotting us."

Again it was worse for those people who lived in town where there were far fewer trees. Derelict buildings, abandoned homes, storage sheds, were all ransacked for anything that could be burned....

"Regular mass attacks are being made on the trees of the island.... whole neighbourhoods declare war over a group of trees, and make havoc with saws and axes.... people are in dire need, and act accordingly."

Diary of Philip Le Sauteur, 4 December 1944

"Elsie says that people in town have got 'wooditis'; I think I've got it too!"

Diary of Nan Le Ruez, 1 January 1945

Even the Black Marketeers started to find life hard as the Occupation dragged onwards, because not even they could find much to sell. The most precious commodity was food, either bought at high price from farmers, or simply stolen. Many noted that people of previously high moral character weren't above trading what little they had to try to put something on the table.

"A.M. Machon was condemned today by Jerry to six months imprisonment, a fine of £300 and some 50,000 marks and £280 of treasury notes were confiscated. All this for selling Black Market pork and butter. The man was Jersey's Black Market King."

Diary of Edward Le Quesne, 19 February 1944

The *Exchange and Mart*, often known as 'For What', was a newspaper advertising service in the *Evening Post*, which became an increasingly popular way for islanders to swap and barter for food, clothing and other essentials.

> "You could advertise what you had – a pair of children's shoes, a pair of men's trousers, 32" waist, good condition, a piece of furniture – and ask what someone might give you in return. Or, as I did, you could ask for something you need before negotiating with whoever might be able to supply it."
>
> Bob Le Sueur, *Growing Up Fast*

What Bob needed in particular shows just how pervasive the shortages were in Jersey. The secretaries in his office had worn the ribbons in their typewriters down to tatters, and they had to be replaced; but there were none in the shops. He finally managed to get some which were not too badly used from a friend.

Bicycle tyres were another example of a mundane item in short supply. As most of the island's cars had been commandeered by the Germans, many islanders were reduced to cycling if they wanted to get anywhere. The occupiers then took many of the island's bikes too, and those that were left fetched astronomical prices at auction. With rubber being an essential war commodity the supply of new tyres to the island stopped very quickly. But as the occupation wore on, tyres wore out; and Jersey people came up with an ideal solution.

They would take an old length of hosepipe and wrap it tightly around the rim of the wheel. Where they met, the ends of the pipe would be clamped together with a metal clip to hold it to the rim and work as an *ersatz* tyre. They were noisy though, and islanders became used to the 'tick, tick, tick' of someone riding towards them. The clips often failed too, resulting in an ignominious fall for the poor rider.

Even Jersey's mighty financial institutions weren't immune to the lack of supplies. Paper, taken for granted everywhere, started to run out. Children were reduced to writing on slates or old cuts of wallpaper because there were no more exercise books, and people re-used envelopes and wrote on both sides of every scrap they could find. It finally caught up with the banks, who ran out of paper on which to print their cheque books.

> "I remember the Midland Bank in particular used to issue cheques which were printed on papers which had been used to cover boxes of island produce before the war. On the reverse side of your cheque to a customer would be all sorts of bright writing all about Jersey tomatoes!"
>
> Bob Le Sueur, *Growing Up Fast*

The diary of Edward Le Quesne, quoted often in this book, was written largely on old tomato packing papers.

Many islanders never forgot the years of want during the Occupation, and appreciated the relative plenty after Liberation when things we might see today as simple pleasures suddenly because available....

"My brother and I were invited to afternoon tea just after Liberation. My
mother said 'You must eat whatever is put in front of you, and say thank you'.
Two bowls were put in front of us, with what looked like a raw egg in the
bottom. My brother nudged me to say 'Come on, you've got to eat this'. I can
still remember the taste of the first spoonful today. It was half a peach in syrup.
It was the most magical thing I have ever tasted. The dear Miss Laurents had
saved that tin for five years for this occasion, and the treat
they gave us was marvellous."
Mary Moody

12 LIBERATION

With the Germans in headlong retreat after the battle of the Falaise Gap in August 1944, there was little doubt that the Allies would win the war and that the Channel Islands would be liberated. The question on everybody's lips was *when?*

Churchill and his military commanders quite rightly realised that the islands held no strategic value at all, in fact quite the opposite as the garrisons there represented thousands of enemy soldiers who could simply be left to their own devices at little threat to the Allied victory. The countless bunkers, guns and tunnels could be left far behind as the British and American armies drove ever eastwards.

As winter approached and supplies dried up, islanders became anxious. While victory seemed certain, would it arrive in time to save them from starvation? Those who still dared listen to their illicit radios followed the inexorable drive towards Berlin, and rejoiced in the positive turn of the fortunes of war. But they did so with empty stomachs, in the cold and dark, with the enemy still all around them.

While the arrival of the *Vega* went some way to alleviating the hunger, they were still uncertain months for people who were still very much under Nazi control. Indeed Hitler appointed a diehard Nazi supporter, Vice-Admiral Friedrich Hüffmeier, to become the new military leader.

Hüffmeier had no intention of surrendering the islands and went from bunker to bunker exhorting his weary, starving troops to prepare to fight.

> "I shall hold out here with you until final victory…. we cannot be shamed
> before the Fatherland, which bears unendingly a much heavier burden than any
> one of us…."
>
> (Quoted from *Jersey Occupied*, Michael Ginns)

German soldiers were often rather less pugnacious. In letters from home they heard of little but defeat, air raids, death and despair, and realised that the end was surely near. What was the point in holding out? While they may not have been facing Russian guns or Allied bombers, they felt cut off from home, and helpless.

Mary Moody's father worked for the Dairy, and collected milk from the island's farmers….

'And our dear Channel Islands are also to be freed today!' - the crowd in the Royal Square listening to Churchill's broadcast on 8 May 1945

The surrender documents are signed on board HMS Bulldog

"One of the soldiers was Fritz, he was 17 and stationed at a gun emplacement near the 'War Tunnels'. He was given a ration of skimmed milk and told my mother he could not eat it as he had heard all his family had perished in the bombing of Berlin and he had nothing to live for.

Later that day we heard a very loud explosion, and the following day Mother was told that Fritz had sat on a keg of gunpowder and placed a hand grenade into his mouth and committed suicide. My mother said 'We are all human, and never let us forget about Fritz.' She always told us to pray for others."

"Being a German soldier in the siege of the islands is far from fun."
Diary of Philip Le Sauteur, 7 April 1945

As Spring brought light and warmth to the islands, the people were cheered by further visits from the *Vega*, and the continued push of the Allied armies. While there was still the fear that Hüffmeier would insist upon a violent end to the Occupation, others were more optimistic.

"Everybody full of hope of an early ending. On Sunday Rev Balleine warned his congregation that they should be ready to attend a thanksgiving for peace at any moment."
Diary of Edward Le Quesne, 2 April 1945

"The war seems to be nearing an end at last. Things are cracking in Germany. What about the poor little Channel Islands? We wait, alternately hoping and fearing. We've been patient so long , that we can remain so a little longer!"
Diary of Nan Le Ruez, 28 April 1945

News from the Front, received on illicit radios that few bothered to hide any longer, told of the collapse of the German armies, the encirclement of Berlin, and eventually the death of Adolf Hitler. German media announced that he had died as a hero, leading the people of Germany.

The surrender soon followed, although there was still uncertainty over whether *Vizeadmiral* Hüffmeier would follow suit in the islands.

On 8th May, the Germans helped to put up several loudspeakers in the Royal Square, and thousands of islanders flocked there to hear the Prime Minister address the nation. Bob Le Sueur watched from a nearby rooftop....

"After announcing the end of hostilities and congratulating the Allies on their success, he uttered the unforgettable news that 'our dear Channel Islands are to be freed today.' The cheer that greeted him was so long and so loud that we missed whatever it was that he said next."

Jubilant crowds and
smiling Tommies;
the delirium
of Liberation

"I think every man, woman and child cried. There wasn't a dry eye in the Square. Strangers were embracing whilst others knelt and prayed."

Len Vautier

"How everyone cheered…. when the Bailiff announced he had been informed that a flotilla of British cruisers and destroyers were approaching the Channel Islands, bringing a British "Commission". How wonderful it was to hear that; we had wondered how they would first come."

Diary of Nan Le Ruez, 8 May 1945

Unfortunately, Mr Churchill was one day early. The excited people who rushed down to the harbour immediately after the broadcast were to be disappointed, as the flotilla of British ships which would take the surrender of the Germans was still en route.

"We are in a state of suspended animation, with the war finished and yet we are still occupied."

Diary of Philip Le Sauteur, 8 May 1945

Nonetheless, there was joy and huge expectation to the extent that few people got a full nights sleep. Many of them, with the Bailiff's encouragement, got out their wireless sets and turned them up full volume to listen to the BBC telling the story of what would become known as 'VE' Day. Union Flags and red, white and blue bunting appeared from nowhere and festooned homes and buildings across the island as word spread of the impending liberation. And the next day, it came.

A DAY TO REMEMBER

9 May 1945 has gone down as perhaps the most joyous in island history. After five long, dark years, the wait was finally over. HMS *Beagle* arrived off the coast of Jersey, and after much sabre rattling the irascible Hüffmeier was persuaded to give up without a fight.

Thousands of expectant islanders gathered around the harbour and cheered as the Bailiff and German officers headed out on a motor launch to the waiting warship where the surrender would be signed. Another boat passed it, heading into the harbour and landing the first British troops to begin the Liberation. There were only two of them. Surgeon-Lieutenant Ronald McDonald and Sub-Lieutenant David Milne were meant to set up communications between the ship and the shore; but the welcome they received meant they found their work very difficult….

"The welcome given to these first British troops to arrive was delirious and hysterical"

Diary of Philip Le Sauteur, 11 May 1945

They were mobbed as they made their way to the Harbour Office in a car, and the place was so packed that they had to get out before they reached their destination. The two men were carried to the building on the shoulders of the cheering crowd and disappeared inside. Moments later they appeared at an upstairs window, and McDonald shouted to make himself heard....

"I really don't know what to say, it has all been too marvellous, everybody on the ship wanted to be the first ashore, and all I can say to you, this has all been too wonderful."

(Quoted from Mark Lamerton, *Liberated by Force 135*)

In what became one of the iconic moments of Liberation Day, he then draped a Union Flag from the window of the office, and more deafening cheers rang out from the starved but ecstatic islanders. But there was more to come.

After the formal surrender had been signed aboard HMS *Beagle*, the main body of liberating troops could come ashore. Twenty soldiers led by Lt. Col. Robinson and Jersey man Captain Hugh Le Brocq, landed from a boat at the New North Quay. They could hardly move for the jostling, cheering, singing crowds who were delirious with happiness. They were kissed, hugged, thanked and mobbed by people who had waited so long for this moment.

"How we cheered and cheered! The soldiers began landing immediately, and as they passed, in single file through the crowds, all who could manage it shook them by the hand and said how pleased we were to see them. The soldiers kissed the children and gave out sweets, chocolate and cigarettes. How wonderful to be there, I'll never forget."

Diary of Nan Le Ruez, 9 May 1945

They managed to fight their way through the crowds towards the Pomme d'Or Hotel, which they were to take over from the Germans as a headquarters. Lt.Col. Robinson noticed that the German flag was still flying from the hotel balcony, and he ordered men to take it down – and replace it instead with the flag that Surgeon-Lieutenant McDonald had unfurled in the Harbour Office. Shortly after half past three Robinson made a short speech to the ever growing crowds gathered in front of the hotel, and raised the flag to a rapturous response. The atmosphere was one of excitement and deep emotion as islanders and Tommies joined in the National Anthem.

The Union Flag flies again

Meanwhile Captain Le Brocq and his men headed up the hill to Fort Regent, where another flag pole was still flying the Swastika. After warning all the Germans inside to get out, he and his men finally took down the enemy flag and raised the red, white and blue to more acclaim from those watching in town below. What a moment for a proud Jerseyman.

Finally the island and its people were free.

Nan Le Ruez remembers a conversation with one of the officers who came ashore….

> "He said 'I have never yet been so very touched as today. I've been there at the Liberation of other countries in West Europe but I've not been so very touched as today, in liberating my own people. It is a privilege to be the first to come, we all wanted to be the first!' What a wonderful day! But how much more wonderful will be the day when I see my Alfred again. That is what I live and long for!"
>
> *Diary of Nan Le Ruez,* 9 May 1945

> "Description of the scenes is impossible – in my mind it is a kaleidoscope of impressions – a lorry load of released Russian prisoners, driven by a German, singing heartily. Released US prisoners happily signing autographs at the Ommarroo Hotel, their new headquarters. A dejected looking 'scuttler' trying to push a wheelbarrow loaded with ammunition through the dense crowds to the assembly dumps. German ships in the harbour painted with the white cross of surrender we had found so galling in 1940. Our troops on the veranda of the Pomme d'Or, throwing cigarettes, chocolate and razor blades to a surging mass of people…."
>
> *Diary of Philip Le Sauteur,* 9 May 1945

Twenty one year old Arthur Shales was one of the crowd outside the Pomme d'Or. As the soldiers stood on the balcony waving, he shimmied up a drainpipe and joined them. Arthur had been a member of the Boys Brigade band before the war, and had managed to keep it going despite a German ban on uniformed organisations. He asked if the band might have the honour of leading a parade through town the next day – an offer which was readily accepted.

> "We stood outside the Pomme d'Or Hotel and saw the Tommies coming through, throwing sweets. I had never seen a sweet before. I didn't get one as there were a lot of people bigger than me."
>
> John Le Gros

"I was sitting on my father's shoulders when the Tommies arrived and one of them handed me some chocolate. I didn't even know what chocolate was…. I looked at my father and asked if I should take it and he said yes. After five years of hardship, I can only describe the taste as heavenly…."

Jeanette Bechelet

While it seemed as though the whole island was there at the Weighbridge on that day of days, there were many who were elsewhere. Farmers and other country folk were busy in their fields while some stayed away for fear of German reprisals.

Bob Le Sueur missed out on it all after an accident that almost cost him his life, and which he has never forgotten. Together with his friends he had ridden down to the harbour to watch the first soldiers arrive. He was just at the bottom of Mount Bingham where there is a small German tunnel….

"Just as I drew level with the tunnel there was an earsplitting BANG! like a gunshot. Two passers-by flung themselves to the ground in alarm, and the two German sentries swung their rifles to aim directly at me as my bike slewed to an ungainly stop….. I looked down, to see the broken and useless piece of hosepipe that had exploded from my front wheel at such an inopportune moment. …. I looked around at the soldiers. One of them seemed to be far younger than I was, perhaps nineteen, and his face broke into a smile before he started to laugh. …. At that moment I wanted more than anything to drop my piece of hosepipe and shake his hand."

Bob Le Sueur, Growing Up Fast

Dejected, Bob pushed his bicycle home and spent the afternoon trying to fix it, missing all the excitement at the Weighbridge. For the rest of his life, he regretted not following his impulse and shaking hands with the defeated foe.

Jersey's prison, not far from the harbour, was still full of islanders who had offended the Germans, some of whom had been lucky not to have been deported to serve their sentence.

Richard Weithley had already escaped once, and was back behind bars when the liberators arrived….

"At around noon on a fine spring morning, I was surprised, astonished and full of hopeful expectation, in that order. Gracie Fields was singing, the sound coming from the direction of the Opera House, over the wall and across the road from the prison. …. less than an hour later, the cell doors were flung open by British soldiers come to our rescue. We were free!"

Richard Weithley: So It Was

For some, the Liberation was a time of mixed emotions. Many had waved goodbye to families and friends five years before and had no news from them since. In the next few days they were able to make inquiries and discover their fates and while many had survived and were in good health, others had not been so lucky. From the joy of being set free from prison, Richard Weithley was soon mourning the death of his brother.

> "My parents were desperately in search of news of my elder brother Middy. News came four days after Liberation. Middy had been killed in action in Hong Kong in 1941. Liberation was of secondary importance, Middy was in everybody's mind. My poor mother, on hearing the news, immediately left the house and was not seen again for eight or nine hours, she had wandered aimlessly with her misery."
>
> Richard Weithley, *So It Was*

Others couldn't resist the temptation of raiding the abandoned German bunkers and tunnels, including Ho8. For many it was a chance to find souvenirs and food....

> "We went down to the bunker at St Catherines and we got knives and forks and plates, sheets and blankets, anything we could carry. I had a blanket on my bed for years with the Organisation Todt colours on it."
>
> Bunny Le Brun

But rooting about in dark tunnels and searching defences for booty could prove dangerous. One young lad was badly injured when he found a gun in an ammunition depot on the New North Quay which went off and hit him in the head and leg. Another young man was hurt when a bullet exploded in the fire at his friend's house.

It was a bad day for women who had been known (or suspected) of associating too closely with the enemy – Jerrybags, guilty of what the French called *Collaboration Horizontale*. Several witnesses describe groups of islanders chasing these unfortunates through the streets and attacking them. Other sympathisers were given short shrift....

> "Several of the more prominent Germanites have sought police protection and are now in gaol, although their premises have been smashed up."
>
> *Diary of Philip Le Sauteur*, 11 May 1945

One of those offered protection was the infamous 'Ginger Lou'. She and her son were kept from vengeful islanders in the prison which until recently had held some of the very people she had denounced. They stayed there for eleven months before being deported and settling in England.

A stern-faced Hüffmeier agrees to come quietly. The rest of the garrison follows him into captivity

Of course, other Jersey people weren't even on the island when it was liberated but were still on the continent. More than six hundred had been held in the castle at Wurzach and had been liberated by British and French forces, without a shot being fired. They were eventually carried back across Europe in a slow and arduous train journey before finally landing in England. There they could celebrate 'VE' Day but for many it took weeks before they could travel back to their island. The future historian Michael Ginns was relieved to be back....

"We arrived home at Les Vars on the 28th August 1945 long after the 9th May Liberation and nothing much in our home had changed.... We had been really lucky, in that the parish Connétable had appointed a fellow parishioner to take care of our property whilst we were interned; so many returned to ransacked houses and their property stolen."

Juanita Shield-Laignel, *Occupation Reconciliation*

For weeks after the Liberation, landing craft came and went from the beach in St Aubin's Bay. They brought troops, machines and supplies, and they took away with them many thousands of Germans. Those that were left were put to work clearing the mines, barbed wire and munitions that had been dug in to surprise any careless enemy; for months the *'Achtung Minen'* signs with their ominous skull and crossbones were still found across the island. Finally they were sent to camps in England before eventually being allowed to return home to Germany.

On 7 June the King and Queen Elizabeth visited the island and spoke to cheering crowds....

"I am confident that , by your endeavours, the destruction wrought by the enemy will soon be repaired and your fields restored to the abundance for which they have so long been famous.
Our thoughts have often been with you in your years of trial."

King George VI

On 22nd June phone links were re-established with Britain.

British military rule lasted for ninety days before the States Assembly was able to take over government of the island once again.

The dark days of Occupation were over.

AFTERMATH

"There were hundreds of Jersey boys who served in the war. Not just in
Normandy, but also in the Far East, in the Air Force, and in the Navy and
Atlantic Convoys, Without the sacrifice that so many Jersey men made, the
island would still be under the Germans, after all."
Billy Reynolds, *Dangerous Driving*

As the spring began a new time of light for Jersey, the island was in a state of
flux. German occupiers were taken away to prison camps, while Jersey people were
returning home.

The internees, who had missed the joyous scenes of Liberation, came back to
an island which had dramatically changed since they last saw it. Whole valleys had
been denuded of trees, huge bunkers and watchtowers dominated the coast, and
the people were gaunt and still trying to come to terms with what had happened
to them. While hunger was nowhere near as bad as it had been a few short weeks
before, food was still rationed and people still had to make do and mend.

Some returned to find their homes had been looted, either by their neighbours
or by the occupiers. Some had even been destroyed entirely to make way for bunkers
or clear fields of fire.

Jersey servicemen who had fought for their King and country also made their
way back as soon as they were released from duty.

Billy Reynolds, who had left with his mother just before the Occupation began,
had joined the army after surviving the Blitz in London and Liverpool. He joined
the same Guards Armoured Division as his brothers and served as an ammunition
lorry driver through the Normandy campaign, in the drive across France and into
the Low Countries. He drove shells across the Nijmegen Bridge under heavy fire,
and rescued a church full of civilians in the fighting on the road to Arnhem. Later
he resupplied tanks in the Battle of the Bulge. Coming home, he reflected on how
the war had changed him....

"It was very strange coming back to our little island. Remember, I had been
away in London, Liverpool and half of Europe before I went home. I remember
very clearly going up Conway Street in St Helier, then turning into New Cut and
thinking 'Oh my God, I didn't realise it was so SMALL!'"

Billy Reynolds, *Dangerous Driving*

Billy went on to have a thriving fish supply business with his family, and remembers how plentiful fish was in the years immediately after the war because so little had been taken during the Occupation.

Clive Kemp, who had lied about his age to join up, had an extraordinary war. After some hasty military training in early 1940 he was sent to a spot near the French border with Belgium to prepare landing strips for RAF fighters. The job didn't last long though, as the Blitzkrieg pushed him and more than three hundred thousand others into the sea at Dunkirk where they were rescued by the famous 'little ships'. Clive would go on to dig for unexploded bombs in the Blitz on London, land on Sword Beach in the first wave on D-Day, build an emergency crossing of the Caen Canal next to the freshly liberated Pegasus Bridge, then build bridges across rivers for tanks and troops from Normandy all the way to Germany.

He expected a hero's welcome when he returned to his island home. But the reality was very different. Some who had endured the Occupation were ready to look down on those who had 'been away', believing they couldn't have suffered the same hardships and privations as they had.

When Clive went to the Housing Department to request somewhere for himself and his wife and newborn child to live, he received a frosty reception from the bureaucrat who saw him....

> "'How many children have you got then?' he asked me. I told him just the one. He looked up from the work he was doing and said 'Well what I'd do if I were you is go back home and make another one. Then I might consider you.'
>
> I wasn't happy at that! I said, 'I've been in the f****ing army since 1939, right through the war, I was at Dunkirk, on the beaches at D-Day, and that's how you treat me?' I told him the place stank, walked out and slammed the door behind me."
>
> Clive Kemp, *Stinkers Nine Lives*

Clive went on to raise his family, worked at the local gas company, and became a founder member of the island's Normandy Veterans Association. He died at the age of 98, and his ashes were scattered at Pegasus Bridge.

Len Samson was another Jersey man with a close connection to that place. In the early hours of D-Day he was one of the brave Paras who jumped into the darkness to take and hold the bridge until the fresh troops could reach them from the beachhead. Landing in a field close to the village of Bénouville he crossed Pegasus Bridge in search of the enemy. Banging on the door of a house, he demanded of the scared inhabitants "Ou est la Boche?!" It is strange to think that both he and Clive Kemp both remembered hearing the bagpipes which heralded the arrival of Lord

Lovat's Commandos to secure the bridge.

After Normandy Len fought in other battles in the liberation of Europe, including the Ardennes. When he finally came home, his first impression was how small his island was.

"The roads looked like they were four inches wide!"

Some of those who had helped escaped slaves gained special recognition from Russia. Several members of the Communist Party in particular, led by Norman Le Brocq, were flown to Moscow and presented with gold watches in gratitude (although most of them stopped working within a few months). Norman went on to become a member of the States and an ardent trade unionist.

Bob Le Sueur and Michael Ginns were both awarded the MBE for their work.

Philip Le Sauteur continued to serve in the states until his death in 1957.

Nan Le Ruez was finally reunited with her fiancée Arthur in England after nearly six years apart. They were married on 13 October 1945.

Edward Le Quesne avoided capture despite sharing the BBC News with trusted customers in his store. In his final diary entry, he thanked his mother for making his Occupation bearable.

Slowly Jersey regained its prosperity through agriculture and tourism. The first anniversary of Liberation was celebrated with joy, and continues to be so.

Every year thousands of people throng the streets of St Helier to mark the occasion, and there is a full ceremony at Liberation Square. It is a poignant place. One of the buildings there bears a plaque commemorating the deportation of more than a thousand islanders in 1942. It is adjacent to the harbour office where Surgeon-Lieutenant Ronald McDonald hung the first Union Flag from the window on Liberation Day, and directly faces the Pomme d'Or hotel from whose balcony Lt. Col. Robinson addressed the crowds. Those momentous events are recreated every 9 May to the cheers of everyone present.

The emotion is palpable, and perhaps the closest we can get to the excitement and joy of that day of all days. The singing of the island song 'Beautiful Jersey' is intensely emotional as people wave their flags with the backing of the Band of the Island of Jersey.

In among the crowd are some with tears in their eyes who still remember those dark years of need and oppression, dwindling in number now but still fiercely proud to have been there. It is always *their* day.

This book is dedicated to them.

7 June 1945. The Bailiff Alexander Coutanche escorts Queen Elizabeth on a visit to the newly-liberated island

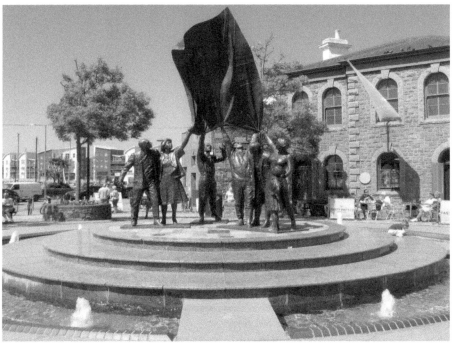

Where it all happened; Liberation Square today

For this book I have tried wherever possible to quote from the accounts of people who actually lived through the Occupation. Some, such as the wonderful diaries of Nan Le Ruez, Edward Le Quesne and Philip Le Sauteur, were written at the time and are very useful in recreating the atmosphere of those long hard years. Published at various times after the war, they paint a clear picture of the drudgery and excitement that characterised Jersey under the jackboot.

Many other memoirs have been published since, some more recently than others, and it is a delight that those two great, irascible Jersey historians Michael Ginns and Bob Le Sueur consented to have their stories told so late in their lives.

Many of the other quotes and comments in the book are directly from the people themselves, recorded during my broadcasting career or simply as valued friends. It was very moving to visit the castle at Wurzach with a handful of the Jersey people who had been interned there, and to look out of its barred windows with them as they reminisced. For them, the years fell away as the memories flooded back.

Books about the Occupation are still published regularly, one of the most significant recently being Therese Tabb's *Occupation Memories* which looks at the war through the eyes of those who were children at the time.

The archives of the *Jersey Evening Post* for the Occupation years are a continuing source of fascination, and easily accessible from the very helpful Jersey Library.

The Jersey Archive has a wealth of information and a helpful website.

There are many other sites to investigate online, but a couple in particular are well worth a visit.

The Frank Falla archive, curated by historian Dr Gilly Carr, has myriad stories of both Jersey and Guernsey people who resisted their occupiers and were punished for it. https://www.frankfallaarchive.org

And 'jerripedia' has stories from many aspects of the island's past, including a lot on the Occupation. https://www.theislandwiki.org/index.php/Jerripedia

Several scholars have attempted to analyse the Occupation, and how islanders and the authorities reacted to it. One of the best known is the controversial *The Model Occupation* by Madeleine Bunting. While many Occupation survivors may take issue with her conclusions, the book performed the important function of making us re-examine some of the established truths about that time.

John Nettles, to whom I am grateful for the foreword to this book, created a deeply researched history of the Occupation entitled *Jewels and Jackboots*, which displays the interest and skills he learned as a history graduate.

There were many other books and sources which proved invaluable, in particular the archives of the Jersey War Tunnels, especially the boxes of unseen photos which were a pleasure to look through. Many of these have been included in this book.

And of course spending hours investigating the tunnels themselves, and experiencing the atmosphere of such an extraordinary place is inspiration enough to want to find out more.

READING LIST
All of these books and publications have been useful in my research for this edition - and every one of them will give readers a new perspective of the Occupation Years:

Booth, Nicholas: *ZigZag* (Portrait, 2007)

Bunting, Madeleine: *The Model Occupation* (Trafalgar Square, 1998)

Channel Islands Occupation Society: *Channel Islands Occupation Review*

Faggione, Gabriele: *Fortifications of the Channel Islands* (CLU, 2013)

Ginns, Michael: *German Tunnels in the Channel Islands* (CIOS, 1993)

Ginns, Michael: *Jersey Occupied* (Channel Island Publishing, 2009)

Jersey War Tunnels: *Guide Book*

Kemp, Clive: *Stinker's Nine Lives* (Seeker Publishing, 2013)

Lamerton, Mark: *Liberated by Force 135* (ELSP, 2000)

Le Quesne, Edward: *The Occupation of Jersey Day by Day*

Le Ruez, Nan: *Jersey Occupation Diary* (Seaflower Books, 1994)

Le Sauteur, Philip: *Diary Of Jersey under The Swastika* (Seeker Publishing, 2017)

Le Sueur, Bob: *Growing up Fast* (Seeker Publishing, 2020)

Le Tissier, Richard: *Island Destiny* (Seaflower Books, 2006)

Macintyre, Ben: *Agent ZigZag* (Bloomsbury, 2007)

McLoughlin, Roy: *Living with the Enemy* (Seeker Publishing, 1995)

McLaughlin, Jean: *Jersey Evacuees Remember* (Channel Island Publishing, 2011)

Nettles, John: *Jewels and Jackboots* (Seeker Publishing, 2015)

Ovenden, John and Shayer, David: *Shipwrecks of the Channel Islands* (Seeker Publishing, 2014)

Reynolds, Bill: *Dangerous Driving* (Seeker Publishing, 2015)

Rothenhäusler, Gisela: *Reaching across the Barbed Wire* (Channel Island Publishing, 2012)

Shield-Laignel, Juanita: *Occupation Reconciliation* (Fish Media, 2017)

Tabb, Therese: *Occupation Memories* (P and T Tabb, 2020)

Weithley, Richard: *So It Was* (Starlight Publishing, 2001)